THE M. & E. HANDBOOK SERIES

MARKETING

F 14

By the same author:

Case Studies in Marketing
Marketing Management

Both published by Macdonald & Evans Ltd.

THE M. & E. HANDBOOK SERIES

MARKETING

G. B. Giles, B.A., Dip.Ed., M.B.I.M., M.Inst.M.

*Head of the Department of Management Studies
Woolwich Polytechnic*

MACDONALD & EVANS LTD
8 John Street, London W.C.1
1969

First published March 1969
Reprinted January 1970
Reprinted March 1971

©

MACDONALD AND EVANS LTD
1969

S.B.N.: 7121 1338 X

 PRINTED BY Unwin Brothers Limited
THE GRESHAM PRESS OLD WOKING SURREY ENGLAND
A member of the Staples Printing Group

GENERAL INTRODUCTION

The HANDBOOK Series of Study Notes

HANDBOOKS are a new form of printed study notes designed to help students to prepare and revise for professional and other examinations. The books are carefully programmed so as to be self-contained courses of tuition in the subjects they cover. For this purpose they comprise detailed notes, self-testing questions and hints on examination technique.

HANDBOOKS can be used on their own or in conjunction with recommended textbooks. They are written by college lecturers, examiners, and others with wide experience of students' difficulties and requirements. At all stages the main objective of the authors has been to prepare students for the practical business of passing examinations.

P. W. D. REDMOND
General Editor

NOTICE TO LECTURERS

Many lecturers are now using HANDBOOKS as working texts to save time otherwise wasted by students in protracted note-taking. The purpose of the series is to meet practical teaching requirements as far as possible, and lecturers are cordially invited to forward comments or criticisms to the Publishers for consideration.

AUTHOR'S PREFACE

THIS HANDBOOK has been written to provide a *vade mecum* for mature students undertaking their first formal course in marketing. It should, therefore, be of special value to those undertaking courses leading to the Diploma in Management Studies, the Higher National Certificate or Diploma in Business Studies and Part 1 of Business Studies degree courses, as well as those preparing for the examinations of the Institute of Marketing, the Advertising Association and certain other professional bodies. Practising businessmen may also wish to have a compact reference book of this kind.

The coverage of subject-matter is extensive but the presentation has been condensed into the form of study-notes for ease of comprehension. In addition to providing a basic framework of study, the HANDBOOK is intended to assist the student in examination revision.

Marketing is a very complex field of study and students should undertake considerable complementary reading to explore in greater depth many of the facets which require more detailed treatment. A list of suggestions for further reading is given in Appendix II. As far as possible the subject should be studied analytically in relation to actual business problems and in this connection the attention of the student is drawn to the author's *Case Studies in Marketing* (also published by Macdonald and Evans).

January 1969

G. B. G.

CONTENTS

Contents

PART ONE
WHAT IS MARKETING ABOUT?

CHAPTER I

MARKETING DEFINED

THE INCREASING IMPORTANCE OF MARKETING

1. Historical development. At the beginning of the Industrial Revolution, Adam Smith in his *Wealth of Nations* said:

> "Consumption is the sole end and purpose of all production; and the interest of the producer ought to be attended to, only so far as it may be necessary for promoting that of the consumer. The maxim is so perfectly self-evident that it would be absurd to attempt to prove it. But in the mercantile system, the interest of the consumer is almost constantly sacrificed to that of the producer; and it seems to consider production, and not consumption, as the ultimate end and object of all industry and commerce."

It was not, however, until the early years of the present century that any serious thought was given by scholars to examining the activities and institutions involved in marketing processes. The practical implications of *consumption being the purpose of production* have only in the last decade or so been recognised by business organisations. As long as the sources and supply of goods were limited and customer demands were comparatively unsophisticated it was possible for a manufacturing company to make profits—and to grow—by concentrating on production efficiency. The customer came at the end of a long chain of events. He was essentially a problem solely for the sales force, whose task was to sell what had been produced. In many cases, particularly with industrial products, it was even believed that goods were bought and not sold, and a reputation built for technical excellence would ultimately lead the customer to seek out the appropriate source of supply.

As production capacity increased and competition became more intense more attention had to be paid to the selling process. Many companies still pay insufficient attention to selling and advertising; others have been forced to devote more and more attention and money to these activities, but often the customer still comes into the reckoning only in the final stages. The disappearance of economic, social, political and technological conditions which make possible an easy sellers' market has brought about in many other companies a complete re-orientation of business philosophy. These companies have adopted or are in the process of adopting *the marketing concept which starts with the customer* in the belief that the most profitable business can only come, as Clive Barwell puts it, "by identifying, anticipating and satisfying customer needs and desires—in that order" A. Wilson (ed.), *The Marketing of Industrial Products*, Chap. I. (Hutchinson, 1965). (*See* also **5** below.)

2. Marketing and change. It may be thought surprising that a concept which was recognised from the very early days of civilisation—as soon as man ceased to be individually self-sufficient and began to make and exchange things with others—and which was enunciated by Adam Smith two hundred years ago—should have been lost sight of, and only recently emerge as new, and even revolutionary. The reason lies in the process of industrialisation itself. At an ever-accelerating rate, Adam Smith's notions of the advantages of specialisation and division of labour spread into all forms of business. The emphasis was not unnaturally, perhaps, placed almost entirely on improving the *productive efficiency* of individually specialised units. Manufacturing specialists dealt with merchant specialists.

New worlds were opened up, populations grew and communications were developed. Soon large-scale operations were needed to satisfy the expanding demand and to capitalise on scientific discoveries and technological progress, as well as to provide economies of scale. Increased output levels required increased levels of consumption. Both combined to produce social change at an unprecedented rate.

3. Major social changes. Amongst the social changes which have been and are still spreading from the earliest Western industrialised societies to all parts of the world, these are the most significant:

(a) *The move from agriculture to industry*; the growth of trade unions and worker co-operation; the increase in white collar workers and salaried staff.

(b) *The provision of greater educational opportunities*; schools, colleges and universities for more and more people, whether rich or poor.

(c) *The raising of living standards*; greater and greater national wealth spread more and more evenly across all levels of national communities; a break-down of traditional class barriers.

(d) *The removal of barriers of distance*; more extensive use of faster and more efficient means of communication.

(e) *The extension of the average life span.*

(f) *The population explosion.*

Sociological changes will take place over the next few decades at an even faster rate, speeded on by technological developments—new materials, greater energy availability, mechanisation and automation, improved information and communication systems.

4. Marketing: A vital business philosophy. It is the greater complexity of the interaction of these various factors of change, the greater speed at which they are taking place, and the greater risks of business investment involved, which make it imperative that the factors of production be organised with as full a prior understanding as possible of the factors of consumption. Marketing thus demands the acceptance of *consumer orientation* by the boards of directors, chief executives, management and employees in every activity. The marketing philosophy then becomes the major driving and co-ordinating force of the whole enterprise.

THE MARKETING FUNCTION

5. Basic marketing activities. The three fundamentals of the marketing function as a whole must be:

(a) the *recognition* and *anticipation* of demand;

(b) the *stimulation* of demand;

(c) the *satisfaction* of demand.

It is the direct responsibility of the chief marketing executive to achieve these objectives, by directing and co-ordinating specific marketing activities, working in co-operation with his fellow executives—manufacturing and purchasing managers for example—under the leadership of the managing director.

6. Organisation of marketing activities. Organisation is itself a means to an end, and its efficiency—necessary for the achievement of that end—depends largely on the clear understanding by those concerned of the elements in the formal organisation structure: *i.e.* authority, responsibility, accountability, and lines of communication.

Organisation of marketing involves both the co-ordination of individual marketing activities *and* the integration of the marketing function with the other functions in the business structure.   Ideally, the task of the marketing manager is as follows:

    (*a*) *He controls directly*:

        (i) marketing research;
        (ii) advertising and sales promotion;
        (iii) sales and distribution;
        (iv) after-sales service.

    (*b*) He is *closely involved in*:

        (i) product planning;
        (ii) product development;
        (iii) public relations and the company image.

7. Qualities needed in a marketing director. It cannot be too much stressed that success depends on the harmonious integration of the whole, as well as the individual parts.   To achieve a profitable balance of products, price, promotion, service and other elements to meet objectives which are in line with the policy and multiple objectives of the Board, marketing executives need more than a drive to achieve current sales volume targets which is the usual objective of sales managers.   They must be capable of objective conceptual forward thinking with the ability to diagnose and analyse problems, and to make plans and see that they are implemented and evaluated.   Experience must be combined with an understanding of economics, behavioural sciences, finance, statistics, mathematics and operational research.

MARKETING THEORY

8. The essence of marketing theory. There are three basic approaches to the study of marketing:

(a) *Institutional analysis.* Marketing institutions are business organisations which are principally concerned with the distribution of goods and services, *e.g.* retailers, wholesalers, advertising and marketing research agencies, commodity exchanges. These institutions have developed because of the separation between producers and consumers. This separation may be one of:

(i) distance;
(ii) time (difference between time of production and time of consumption need); or
(iii) knowledge.

In addition organisations such as banks, hire purchase and insurance companies function as marketing institutions when they provide services that facilitate the flow of goods from producer to consumer.

(b) *Functional analysis.* Marketing functions may be described as major marketing operational activities, *e.g.* pricing, selling, advertising.

(c) *Commodity or channel of distribution analysis.* A study of channels of distribution would involve tracing the passage of individual products or commodities through various marketing institutions from producer to consumer, investigating the functions performed at each stage.

It is important for students to understand the three basic approaches that are combined in this book.

9. The relevance of economics. In order to understand each of the three basic approaches and their inter-relationships it is necessary to draw on relevant concepts of economics. A study of economic aggregates, *i.e.* total consumption, total income, total employment, is described as *macro-economics* and this branch of study has relevance to marketing; *e.g.* demand for goods and services may be subject to external constraints imposed by government economic policy or wage levels. A study of the economy in detail, *e.g.* how prices of goods are determined, what factors determine the quantity and type of goods produced, is described as *micro-economics* and has very special significance for the marketing student. The application of micro- and macro-economics may be seen in the case of the demand for television sets, which may be affected by such considerations as the price, the hire purchase facilities available, the number of producers and distributors, government taxation policy and technological development.

10. The relevance of behavioural sciences. Production, marketing and consumption are carried on by human beings whose attitudes and decisions are the result of psychological or sociological influences which may be in conflict with rational economic motives. Marketing students must, therefore, make use of relevant concepts of the behavioural sciences.

11. The relevance of statistics, mathematics and finance. Marketing is concerned with the allocation of scarce resources to achieve profit and growth objectives in the market place. The marketing student should therefore learn to assess and control, wherever possible, in quantitative terms, input and output. He must consequently become familiar with the relevant branches of statistics, mathematics and finance.

12. The approach of this book. Because of the complexity of real marketing situations an inter-disciplinary approach has been taken in this text. Institutions, functions and channels will be studied against a background of interacting and changing technical, economic and cultural conditions. In the remainder of Part I we shall first look at the key figure in this complex—the customer—and examine ways of understanding him better by means of marketing research. Part II is concerned with planning, distributing and communicating in such a way that customer and company goals are satisfied. Part III is devoted to the operational strategy, organisation and control which are essential for growth, and even survival, in dynamic marketing conditions.

PROGRESS TEST 1

1. What major social changes have contributed to the need for companies to be marketing oriented? **(3)**
2. What are the three basic activities of the marketing function? **(5)**
3. What are marketing institutions and what functions do they perform? **(8)**

CHAPTER II

CONSUMER BEHAVIOUR

STAGES IN THE DECISION PROCESS

1. Outline of the decision process. Consumer behaviour is determined by economic, psychological and sociological considerations. It is important to study non-economic buying motivations as these are present in the buying of industrial goods and services as well as in consumer purchases.

The process of decision may be long in duration, as in the decision to buy a computer, or short, as in the decision to buy a packet of sweets, but similar stages may be observed:

(*a*) A general or a specific need is felt (*see* **2-5**).

(*b*) A period of pre-buying activity follows, *i.e.* an investigation of sources of supply which might satisfy the need (*see* **6**).

(*c*) A decision is taken (what to purchase, or even to make no purchase) based on the results of the pre-buying activity and the strength of the need (*see* **7**).

2. The basic need. This may be either *general, e.g.* I need a change of environment, or *specific, e.g.* I need a holiday in Spain. The more specific need may arise spontaneously or it may be stimulated by creative marketing. The basic need is for a collection of utilities providing a psychological or social satisfaction and not for a product. Consequently, it is important that marketing programmes should be designed to identify products or services giving satisfaction of a need. A classification of basic needs is set out in **3-5** below.

3. Psychological needs. These cover the following:

(*a*) *The physiological*—the need to satisfy the bodily requirements, *e.g.* of hunger, thirst.

(*b*) *Pleasure satisfaction*—physical and aesthetic, appeals to the senses. Certain foods have a pleasurable flavour; certain furnishings bring aesthetic satisfaction.

(*c*) *Security*—the need to protect oneself from danger or worry.

(d) *Ownership*—the innate drive to possess things.

(e) *Self-esteem*—the desire to satisfy the "ego."

4. Sociological needs. These include the following:

(a) *Love of others*—particularly those in close family relationship.

(b) *Social acceptance*—the need to be recognised by the many formal and informal groups to which a person belongs. This need may be to conform or to be distinctive.

5. The hierarchy of needs. Some of these needs are stronger than others at particular times, in particular people, and in particular societies. It will also be apparent that some of these needs are closely linked with others. Maslow has set out a five-stage priority of human needs, the first two of which are primary needs fundamental to existence, the last three secondary:

(a) Basic physiological needs (conditions affecting the human body—hunger, sleep, temperature).

(b) Safety needs (self-protection against present and future dangers).

(c) The need for recognition, for love and belonging.

(d) Ego-satisfying needs (desire for self-esteem, self-respect).

(e) Self-fulfilment needs (realisation of complete self, creativity). This need is felt and satisfied by relatively few.

See A. H. Maslow, *Motivation and Personality* (Harper and Row, New York, 1954).

6. Pre-buying activity. No two people "perceive" things in exactly the same way. Past experiences, the way in which one's senses have been stimulated, condition one's attitude towards objects, words and ideas. Accumulated experience builds up, over a period of time, a perceptual framework so that one has a predisposition to see or believe what one expects or would like to see or believe. Once a buying need is felt the perceptual framework is more vigorously activated and motivated at a conscious and subconscious level. The potential buyer's ultimate decision is now more likely to be influenced by advertising, displays, or personal sales talks, or by other people's attitudes and opinions. This pre-purchase activity can be broken down into six changes as follows:

    (*a*) Awareness.
    (*b*) Knowledge.
    (*c*) Liking.
    (*d*) Preference.
    (*e*) Conviction.
    (*f*) Purchase.

7. The decision complex. The decision itself is really a result of a collection of decisions, *e.g.* what class of product, what type or brand, what design, what quantity, in what place, from whom, at what price, by what method of payment. One of the tasks of marketing is to communicate with the potential buyer in such a way that not only does he become aware of the existence of the product or service offered, but develops such a sufficiently strong and favourable attitude that he will go through the buying decision processes with a greater degree of confidence. Uncertainty and delay in making buying decisions is often the result of a conflict between rational economic motives and non-rational external and internal stimuli. So-called "impulse" buying is more frequently found where there is no economic anxiety—with comparatively inexpensive, frequently purchased products, for example where non-rational external stimuli (packaging, promotions, display) have a major influence.

MAJOR MARKETING STIMULI

8. The product. As has been pointed out, a product may represent economic utility to a purchaser. He may, for example, believe an electric drill will save the expense of hiring outside labour to make improvements to his house. The purchase of an electric drill, however, may not arise from purely economic motives. The prime urge may be to gain the admiration of others. Even if there are economic motives these will be modified by the system of values of the individual and of the social environment which influences his attitudes and behaviour. The more affluent the society, the greater the spread of disposable income (money available after essential purchases have been made), the greater is the problem of choice. The choice is not simply between various types and makes of drills but between drills and a whole collection of completely different items such as holidays, refrigerators, furniture, between buying now or saving. Similarly, choice between drills of different designs, performance and price depends on interacting economic, psychological and sociological motivations.

9. The package. Packaging materials, design, colour, size, illustrations, brand names and associated symbols (logotypes), type faces, copy and lay-out may affect to a very considerable extent a potential buyer's perception of a product. Packaging plays a vital role in stimulating memory and helping recognition, gaining shelf space and attracting the eye, providing use, storage and transportation benefits, but it has wider behavioural implications in terms of establishing customer preference.

10. Price. The level at which a firm sets its prices will affect both sales and profitability. The demand for a car at £4000 will be smaller than that for a car at £800. Under certain circumstances, it may be more profitable for a particular company to concentrate on the more limited demand market. From the basic economic law of supply and demand (*i.e.* the lower the price, the greater the quantity of demand) it is possible to construct graphs of theoretical demand quantities in relation to price. Some products will be seen to have much greater price elasticity than others, *e.g.* the demand for a breakfast cereal might be reduced by one-tenth if prices were doubled while the demand for a toilet soap might be cut by 70% by a similar price change. It is important to study price elasticity considered in conventional economic terms, such as availability of substitutes, durability and ability to postpone purchase, income, population and the prices of competing products. It is also important to realise that in developed economics psychological aspects of pricing take on greater and greater significance. Low price, for example, may be irrationally associated with poor quality (*see* Chapter V).

11. The promotion. Many advertising campaigns are mainly planned in quantitative terms. How many people will be exposed to what weight of advertising during what period of time? To this quantitative thinking is added a target audience defined in broad socio-economic categories. The most common measurements of effectiveness are based on recall (*i.e.* recollection of advertisements), but recall may be utterly unrelated to purchasing activity (*see* VII, **9–10**).

Advertising and communications must be directed towards stimulating favourable trade opinions and feelings about a company as well as favourable customer attitudes towards product quality, price, delivery, sales and technical services. Concepts derived from clinical research and the findings of sociologists, psychologists and anthropologists may be used to determine why people buy particular products or services, and lead to advertising which appeals to needs, wants and desires, so that potential buyers may rationalise the desire to buy, *e.g.* a ten-year guarantee originally given with mopeds in Germany inhibited sales since many potential customers had guilt feelings about buying a product they would expect to exchange for a car in two or three years. Advertising copy and visual elements are therefore designed in the light of anticipated connotations, *i.e.* the mental images aroused in the reader or viewer beyond what is superficially or explicitly expressed.

In marketing a product it is certainly important that the product itself, the packaging, the price and the promotion should have a consistent appeal in terms of the attitudes and motivations of potential buyers. This calls for deliberate research and planning.

THE INFLUENCES OF PERSONALITY AND ENVIRONMENT

12. Social influences. While personality conditions a buyer's behaviour in an individual way according to his personal aspirations, temperament and philosophy, cultural and organisational influence also have a profound effect. Cultural differences are brought about by the sets of values to which individuals have been exposed from birth, *e.g.* as a child at home, as a pupil in a particular school environment, etc. Other social influences later are brought to bear. The organisation in which people work is a social institution where irrational values develop. This complex of influences is brought to bear on both consumer and industrial buying.

It would be impossible to devise a marketing programme to meet every individual circumstance and it is important, therefore, to identify significant group behavioural patterns. Consistent spending patterns may, for example, be related to the following variables:

    (*a*) Urban and rural communities.
    (*b*) Family income levels.
    (*c*) Occupations.
    (*d*) Education.
    (*e*) Age.
    (*f*) Sex.
    (*g*) Informal social group membership.
    (*h*) Race or nationality.
    (*i*) Religion.

13. Dangers of conventional market profiles. The problem then is to examine the behavioural patterns which emerge from combinations of those variables listed above and to uncover the underlying and not merely the superficial rationalisations of attitudes, and to determine which patterns are really significant.

There is a tendency to generalise in terms of a single variable.

Many American manufacturers, for example, have assumed that the discount store appeals only to lower and middle income groups, but research has shown that in New York 70% of all women buy some goods from discount stores and 12% of those in higher income groups do more than half their shopping there. Some shops and brands—and especially the former—provide satisfaction which leads to strong loyalties, and indeed many women rely on the reputation of the store in judging quality and value in the case of certain items. The importance of *informal* group influence therefore becomes more evident—and informal groups may have very varying degrees of homogeneity in relation to occupation, family income, education, and so on. Traditional demographic means of segmenting markets must be modified. An elementary study of demand patterns for, say, cars, shampoos, vans, computers or watches will show the danger of relying entirely on standardised socio-economic layer theories.

14. Customer attitudes and behaviour. In order to understand behaviour it is necessary to find out why people act in certain ways, why they hold certain opinions and have developed certain attitudes. Having discovered basic physical characteristics of markets, *e.g.* how many people they comprise, the level of earnings, the level of spending on various types of products and services, it is essential to discover why and how people have acted as they have. Marketing is concerned with change, adapting to change and creating change. Current and historic spending and saving patterns may provide a basis for market prediction, but a healthy sales and profit record for a product which has represented the best rationalised compromise available of needs and their satisfaction may be of little avail if a product much more near the customer's perception of the ideal becomes available.

15. The corporate image. A potential buyer's attitude to a product may be modified by his attitude to the organisation which manufactured the product. A retailer may be more ready to handle a new product from a manufacturer whose products have yielded good profits in the past. A potential user may choose a plane of a particular brand because he has had good service from a saw made by the same manufacturer. In view of the fact that most companies now manufacture and/or market a wide range of products or services, increasing attention is being paid to the development of corporate images which are aimed at creating a widespread favourable company identification or image by means of advertising, public relations, factory design, product design, stationery, transport and so on. Corporate image building is aimed not solely at potential customers but also at other individuals and institutions on which future prosperity may depend, for example:

(*a*) shareholders and potential investors;
(*b*) the government;
(*c*) employees;
(*d*) suppliers;
(*e*) the public in the immediate vicinity of company premises;
(*f*) schools and universities from which staff may be recruited.

INDUSTRIAL BUYING BEHAVIOUR

16. Buying motives. Many products are bought as part of a total system; for example, even a domestic detergent is part of a system involving the whole organisation of the housewife's tasks and, in particular, is related to problems of time and equipment (*e.g.* washing machine) available, apart from its fitness for a particular purpose.

It is more commonly *industrial products* which are consciously thought of by buyers *as part of a total system.* Materials, components and machines fit into a manufacturing process system and change will react upon the whole system. Therefore, in marketing the product it is necessary to consider not only the functioning of the whole system, but also the subjective behaviour and values of people likely to be affected by change. Constructional materials for example, must be functionally compatible with other products in the system and be acceptable to architects, engineers, contractors, as well as being compatible with the human and mechanical resources available. There is, indeed, a growing movement towards systems selling! This may involve a product which incorporates a number of functions, *e.g.* the combined harvester or the computer. In large-scale contracts it is sometimes an advantage for companies to combine to present a total system, *e.g.* to construct an electricity power station.

17. The industrial buying complex. Successful industrial marketing requires that very special attention be paid to discovering the following:

  (*a*) *Who* the buyers are.
  (*b*) *Where* they are.
  (*c*) *How* they may be reached.
  (*d*) *What* they really want.
  (*e*) What *motives* will induce them to buy.

It should not be assumed that industrial products cannot be differentiated and that success or failure depends only on a single combination of the right specifications, price and delivery. In the most non-differentiated commodity situations a whole range of differentials is possible, *e.g.* better technical advice, more frequent or regular delivery. The way in which buyers "perceive" a problem (*see* **6**) can change. Technology changes, company policy changes, company organisation changes.

18. Specific behavioural questions. Key questions to be answered when marketing industrial products are the following:

(a) *When repeated purchases are made, are they regarded as a major new decision* each time or as a re-buying situation?

(b) *How is a "re-buy" or a "new buy" situation handled* in terms of the decision process?

(c) *Who are the major buying influences* in various situations? Who plays a key role and when?

(d) *What are the major motivations* of these decision-makers and executives of key influence likely to be in particular situations? These motivations will not be entirely rational. There will be different formal and informal relationships, different environmental backgrounds, training and interests.

(e) *What is the effect of the formal and informal organisational structure on buying behaviour?* The reward system, the status system, the authority system and the communications system, the extent of centralisation—all have an important bearing (*see* X, **2, 15**). Good industrial salesmen know intuitively that buyers are subject to normal human anxieties, frustrations, inertia. A more scientific study of behaviour would improve not only the effectiveness of the salesman, but the effectiveness of the whole consumer-oriented marketing operation.

PROGRESS TEST 2

1. What is meant by "the hierarchy of needs"?   (**5**)

2. By what four major stimuli might a marketing organisation stimulate customer demand?   (**8–11**).

3. What are some of the social and economic group factors to be considered in examining buying patterns?   (**12**)

4. Why is it necessary to develop a corporate image?   (**15**)

5. What is systems selling?   (**16**)

CHAPTER III

MARKETING RESEARCH

MARKETING RESEARCH AND DECISION-MAKING

1. Decisions and Risk. Marketing decisions are inevitably made under conditions of uncertainty. Uncertainty involves both risk and opportunity. The use of marketing research does not and cannot eliminate either risk or opportunity, but its intelligent use can reduce risk and indicate the degree of probability of the various possible outcomes of opportunity. Markets are increasingly dynamic and competitive; their successful exploitation calls for greater investment, and more frequent innovation. Decision-making, therefore, must be faster and less susceptible to many of the needless errors of intuitive judgment.

2. Marketing research: Definition and application. Marketing research may be defined as the objective and systematic collection, recording, analysis, interpretation and reporting of information about: existing or potential markets (*i.e.* market research, **5**), marketing strategies and tactics, and the interaction between markets, marketing methods and current or potential products or services (*see* **4-7**). It can therefore play a major role in enabling the modern executive to apply a truly analytical approach to decision-making. It can also assist in the evaluation of the effect of decisions which have been taken.

3. Origin and development. Marketing research has a comparatively recent origin, the first formal marketing research organisation having been established in the United States in 1911. From slow beginnings, in recent years, there has been a growing sophistication in methods and methodology (*see* **17**, market research process)—in the application of statistical techniques and behavioural science concepts (*see* **34** below)—and the early scepticism of managements and the sometimes exaggerated claims of pseudo-researchers are rapidly disappearing. The use of marketing research in consumer markets is now reasonably widespread. The need for the objective evidence which marketing research as a decision-making tool can provide for management in producer goods or industrial markets is probably even greater than in consumer goods markets, but its value in these areas has been too little realised and research activity has consequently been more limited (*see* XI, 5).

THE SCOPE OF MARKETING RESEARCH

4. Marketing research and management problems. In the following paragraphs (5–7) are some examples of the enormous range of problems on which management may require information, whether on the markets for their products (or services), or marketing strategy, or on the products themselves seen in this context of markets and marketing methods.

5. Markets. An up-to-date knowledge of the market is essential for successful marketing. Management must ask themselves the following questions:

(*a*) What is the *size* of a market for a product or service (in terms of volume and/or value)?

(*b*) What is the past *pattern of demand*; what factors (economic, social, political, technological) might affect future demand and when? Is demand subject to seasonal or cyclical variations?

(*c*) What is the *market structure*; *e.g.* is it based on industry, on size or numbers of companies, on income groups, on sex, on age, on geographical distribution?

(*d*) What are the *buying habits*, motivations, procedures, of domestic customers, retailers, wholesalers, professional and industrial buyers?

(*e*) What is the company's *market share* and how does this compare with competitive shares over various time periods?

(*f*) What are past and future *trends*—rate of change in population, national income, retail sales, industry output?

(*g*) Which *overseas markets* present the best immediate or long-term opportunities?

6. Marketing policy and strategy. Armed with a knowledge of the market, management can consider their overall marketing policy and tactics. They will require further information about competition, costs, and the probable results of different courses of action, *e.g.*:

(*a*) Where, how and at what cost do competitors advertise? What are competitive pricing structures and practices?

(*b*) How do marketing and distribution costs compare, in total and by individual elements, with competitive costs?

(*c*) What are the most effective channels of distribution?

(*d*) How do sales differ by territory, industry, type of outlet, and why?

(*e*) What effect on demand will there be if a new product is introduced under an established corporate image or a separate brand name?

(*f*) What would be the effect of a change in pricing structure, on the number and frequency of orders, or on factory and store inventory levels?

(*g*) What amount of service, at what cost, is it necessary to provide to maintain or improve profitability?

(*h*) What is the effect of sales promotional activity?

7. Products and services. The third factor to be considered is the product itself, in terms of suitability for the market, design and manufacture, competitive advantages and profitability, *i.e.*:

(*a*) What is the company reputation or image, for products, presentation, technical service, delivery? What are the major weaknesses of products—own and competitive?

(*b*) How are products/services used and what characteristics are considered most important? What should be the range offered, *e.g.* prices, sizes, colours, designs?

(*c*) What changes will be necessary in materials used, advantages offered, functions performed, and when? Should certain products be dropped and when?

(*d*) What is the best pricing structure for a new product? What might be the effect on the profitability of a product or volume sales of a price increase of, *e.g.* 4%?

(*e*) What patents, licensing agreements or other legal restrictions might affect manufacture or sale of a product?

(*f*) What do reactions to products in test markets indicate in terms of national or international operations?

8. Marketing research and company organisation. The range of studies which the marketing researcher may be asked to undertake extends across departmental or functional barriers. Examples of studies in which executives other than those in marketing divisions would be concerned are as follows:

(a) Plant location studies.
(b) Economic forecasting in connection with budgets.
(c) Studies of companies under consideration for acquisition.
(d) Analysis of transport utilisation.

In any company organisation, marketing research must therefore be placed under the control of an executive who is sympathetic to its importance, its need for adequate finance and its essential objectivity (it must be protected from personal pressures to find support for the subjective judgments of management). The data and recommendations produced should be regularly and easily available to appropriate decision and policy makers, whether they be individuals or committees. In small companies, ideally a marketing research manager should report to the chief executive. In large companies, with a marketing director at policy-making level, marketing research might report to that executive. Many companies have no marketing research staff of their own, but too frequently when specialist staff is employed, its effect is negligible because it is too remote from major decision centres. (Where company marketing research departments do exist, they are usually small and a number of projects are assigned to outside independent agencies.)

9. Dangers in use of terminology. Specialists in marketing research departments must combine skills from economics, psychology, sociology, mathematics and statistics. One of the major dangers is that these specialists should forget that their prime aim is to assist in the solution of marketing problems and become to involved in research methodology (*see* **17(a)**, **43**) for its own sake. Personal communications with other executives and final research reports can be hampered by an over-emphasis on technical terminology. Findings and methods should be explained in language non-specialists can understand.

SOURCES OF INFORMATION

10. Data types. Data is generally classified as either primary or secondary.

B

(*a*) *Primary data.* This is information which has originated directly as a result of the particular problem under investigation.

(*b*) *Secondary data.* Data which already exists and may be used for an investigation but has not been collected for that specific purpose is called *secondary data.* It is usually cheaper to use this kind of data than to set up special investigations, but care must be taken to ensure that the data is relevant, can be adjusted to the problem, and is reliable.

11. Sources of secondary data. These can be divided into internal and external sources.

(*a*) *Internal.* There is invariably a mass of marketing information in a company's own records—particularly sales records. This information may not have been collected systematically or in a readily appropriate form, but it is clear that marketing researchers should turn first to the sources which, properly organised, can provide continuously relevant current data as well as information for occasional and special investigations. Data-processing equipment, computers and the systems approach are making the extrapolation of appropriate information easier and faster.

(*b*) *External.* In addition there is a wealth of published information available from external sources, *e.g.* agencies, consultants, Government departments, trade associations, banks, professional bodies, research organisations, the press. Some of these are outlined in paragraphs **12–16** below. A fuller list of various bodies and publications which provide useful information is given in Appendix I.

12. Specialist marketing research agencies. Large numbers of these agencies, varying enormously in size and specialisation exist in the UK and in many parts of the world. The larger agencies usually offer a wide range of services but some concentrate on projects requiring more specialised skills, *e.g.* field interviewing in connection with industrial markets, motivation research, research connected with specific industries.

Special services offered by agencies include the following:

(*a*) The *A.C. Nielsen food and drug indices* which provide extensive data at frequent intervals obtained from a large sample (*see* **21** below) of product sales by brand, retail purchases, inventory levels and movement, retail and wholesale prices, percentage distribution, etc. Data is broken down in various ways, *e.g.* by geographical area, type of store.

(b) The advertising research services of the *Gallup* and *Starch organisations*. Gallup tests advertising research in mass circulation printed media, while Starch attempts to evaluate whether particular current advertisements are or will be read more than past advertisements or competitive advertisements.

(c) The *Audit Bureau of Circulation*, an organisation set up by publishers to provide certified information on the circulation of printed media. It should be noted that many specialist magazines do not subscribe to the Audit and there is no objective measurement of circulation figures claimed.

(d) *Measurement of television audiences*. Independent Television Audiences were measured by Television Audiences Measurement (TAM) up to the end of July 1968, when Audits of Great Britain (AGB) began a five-year contract awarded by the Joint Industry Committee for Television Audience Research (JICTAR). Both agencies use electrical devices fitted to a sample of sets in the 14 television areas. The TAM system depended on visiting 2120 homes to collect information. AGB statistics are derived from paper tape recordings indicating when receivers are switched on and off and when a channel change is made. The tapes are posted by the housewives of the 2650 homes where AGB meters have been fitted. The AGB system enables agencies and advertisers to obtain faster and more detailed information. Problems of more refined measurement, *e.g.* the numbers of persons watching particular programmes or advertisements, their reactions and subsequent buying behaviour, are as yet unsolved.

13. Advertising agencies. The demands of clients for more comprehensive marketing information as part of a total marketing plan, together with the growing need for agencies to be competitive, has led to a considerable extension of marketing research departments in advertising agencies. The cost of sustaining these services is leading more often to an additional charge above the 15% commission on which agencies have traditionally operated (*see* VI, **22**).

14. Advertising media proprietors and contractors. Much of this research is basically intended to show the effectiveness of the particular media being sold and great care is needed in interpreting the studies. Nevertheless, the practice of producing such research data is gaining ground rapidly and much of the information may be free from promotional bias (*see* VI, **24**).

15. Trade associations. Studies are usually very limited in scope and statistics may be difficult to interpret if important companies or groups of companies are omitted. However, studies which are available are particularly useful in industrial marketing research, where there is a comparative lack of sources of secondary data (*see* Appendix 1).

16. Government departments and international organisations. These are invaluable research sources; British government departments provide both annual and monthly statistics on many topics, and foreign governments provide information through their embassies or issue bibliographical lists from the appropriate trade ministers. Other statistics are published by various international bodies, *e.g.* UNO, OECD.

Some of the great number of reports available are listed in Appendix I.

EXECUTING MARKETING RESEARCH STUDIES

17. Steps in the market research process. Research projects are not susceptible to any one complete and inflexible sequence of steps and the type of problems to be studied will determine the particular steps to be taken and their order. The following steps provide, however, a useful procedural guide:

(*a*) *Definition of the problem.* This step is of the greatest importance. Frequently management initially poses an ill-defined problem or one which is a superficial aspect of a more fundamental problem. Care must be taken to verify the objectivity and validity of the background facts and to agree upon the problem in writing with the executive or executives concerned with its circumstances.

(*b*) *Specification of the information required.*

(*c*) *Design of the research project,* involving consideration of:

(i) the means of obtaining the information;

(ii) the availability and skills of company marketing research staff and/or agencies;

(iii) methodology; *i.e.* a detailed explanation of the way in which selected means of obtaining information, *e.g.*

observation studies, questionnaires, will be organised, and the reasoning leading to the selection.

(iv) the time and cost of the research.

(d) *Sample design.*

(e) *Construction of questionnaires* and/or preparation of briefs for field interviews.

(f) *Execution of the project,* with arrangement for checks on the reliability of data being collected.

(g) *Analysis of data.*

(h) *Preparation of report and recommendations.*

18. Sampling. When field studies are undertaken considerations of time and cost almost invariably lead to contact being made with a selection of respondents. The respondents selected should be as representative as possible of the total population to be investigated in order to produce a miniature cross-section. The selection process is called sampling. The word "universe" is often used to describe the whole population from which the selection is made. Samples are of two basic types:

(a) *Probability or random samples;* samples which are so constructed that every element from the total population has a known probability of selection and the limits of probable error in relating results to the whole population are thus known mathematically in advance.

(b) *Non-probability or purposive samples;* samples based on the choice of the selector.

19. Comparison of probabilities and non-probability samples. Probability samples enable experimental error to be measured but they do not necessarily provide more accurate marketing research results than non-probability samples. A small probability sample may yield a high experimental error; even with a large sample, errors may arise because of variability in the characteristics of the population being examined, *e.g.* attitudes, habits. Non-probability samples are subject to error in sample selection, but the risk of selection bias has to be weighed against the risk of experimental errors arising from smaller probability samples. In industrial marketing research, executive judgment is likely to be more accurate than in consumer marketing research because of a more exact knowledge of a comparatively small universe. Concepts of probability are frequently used in non-probability samples and judgment is applied to give "weighting" to factors according to their likely importance.

20. Modified probability samples. Statisticians have developed a number of specialised probability procedures which are of particular value in marketing research. The most significant are considered in 21–25 below.

21. Systematic sampling. Only the first unit of the sample is selected at random. The following units are selected at fixed intervals. If, for example, questions were to be asked of householders in a road and the 3rd house were selected randomly as the starting point, there would be systematic sampling if subsequent interviews were carried out at fixed regular intervals, *e.g.* at the 8th, 13th, 18th, 23rd house and so on. The cost can be controlled by the intervals selected. The basic assumption is that all elements of the population are ordered in a manner representative of the total population. A systematic sample of a list of customers arranged according to their annual purchases would meet this assumption, whereas there is a possibility that every fifth customer entering a store on a given day may be unrepresentative of the weekly clientele.

22. Stratified sampling. If there is evidence that certain elements of the population are more significant for the purpose of a survey than others it may be desirable to weight these elements in proportion to their significance. If, for example, tea consumption of a household were significantly related to family size and particular age groups, a stratified sample would give due weighting to respondents who conformed to the significant criteria. Stratified samples may be especially useful in industrial marketing research if, for example, volumes of output or number of employees are known significant factors. Interviewers are sometimes instructed to survey fixed proportions to a given population, *e.g.* 50% of large firms in a given geographical area. This is described as *quota sampling*. This technique is not based on probability and is susceptible to interview bias in selection.

23. Cluster and area sampling. Geographical dispersal of interviews creates cost problems. Cluster sampling reduces cost by concentrating surveys in selected clusters, *e.g.* particular sales areas, counties, local authority areas, towns. The principle of statistical random selection could be applied in the selection of clusters and units within the clusters. Clusters may be selected on the basis of predetermined strata, *e.g.* if home ownership is an important factor it may be necessary to identify clusters according to known data on home ownership.

24. Multi-stage sampling. This is a development of the principle of cluster sampling. The first stage may be to select large primary sampling units, *e.g.* counties, then towns and finally districts within towns.

25. Sequential sampling. This is a complex technique. The ultimate size of the sample is not fixed in advance but is determined according to mathematical decision rules on the basis of information yielded as surveys progress.

26. Methods of collecting data. Data can be collected either through observation or through direct communication with respondents, whether by mail, telephone or personal interview. The advantages and disadvantages of these methods are outlined below (**27–28**).

27. Observation. The observation method is most commonly used in studies of consumer behaviour in stores.

  (*a*) *Advantages*.

    (*i*) If the observer records accurately, subjective bias is eliminated (direct communication methods bear the note of bias either in questioner or in respondent).

    (*ii*) Information relates to what is currently happening; it is not complicated by consideration of past behaviour, future intentions or attitudes.

  (*b*) *Disadvantages*.

    (*i*) It is usually an expensive method.

    (*ii*) Information provided is very limited.

28. Mailing and questionnaires. This is the method most extensively employed (*see* also **33** below).

(a) *Advantages*.

    (i) Low cost even when spread widely geographically.

    (ii) Lack of interviewer bias.

    (iii) Some respondents are difficult to interview—particularly in industrial markets.

    (iv) Respondents have more time to give considered answers.

    (v) Respondents may prefer anonymity.

(b) *Disadvantages*.

    (i) Limitation of information. To be successful questionnaires should be comparatively short and simple. Questions may be dichotomous (yes-or-no answers), multiple choice (alternative answers listed), or open-ended. The latter are often difficult to analyse. A specialised form of multiple choice questions involves *scaling*. For example, respondents may be asked to rank products in order of preference or to indicate an attitude according to its strength, say from "like very much" to "dislike intensely." One of the problems arising from scaling questionnaires is the difficulty of establishing the exact intervals; for example, are products 1 and 2 seen to be more nearly equal than 4 and 5?

    (ii) Problems of having constantly up-dated mailing lists.

    (iii) Low rate of return and the difficulty of knowing whether willing respondents are truly representative. Sometimes a number of personal field interviews or telephone enquiries are carried out to check on the validity of the sample of questionnaires actually returned. It should be noted that the rate of return will depend on such factors as the skill of questionnaire construction and time of mailing.

    (iv) Possible ambiguity of replies or omission of replies to particular questions.

    (v) Inflexibility; difficulty of amending the approach once questionnaires have been despatched. Pilot testing is, in any case, very desirable to avoid question construction faults which may lead to answers which defy analysis.

NOTE: Questionnaires should contain "control" questions which indicate the reliability of the respondent. For example, a question designed to determine consumption of particular materials may be asked first in terms of financial expenditure and later in terms of weight. Again, one or two questions not directly related to the purpose of the survey may produce answers which cast doubt on the reliability of the respondent.

29. Telephone interviews. Although this method has

many advantages, particularly in industrial surveys, it is not used as widely in the UK as might now be expected.

(a) *Advantages*

    (i) More flexible than mailing.

    (ii) Interviewer can explain requirements more easily.

    (iii) Faster than other methods.

    (iv) Cheaper than personal interviewing.

    (v) Ease of re-call.

    (vi) Access can sometimes be gained to respondents who would neither be interviewed personally nor answer questionnaires.

    (vii) Replies can be recorded without embarrassment to respondent.

    (viii) Higher response rate than from mailing.

    (ix) Useful for radio and television surveys when checking programmes actually being heard or viewed.

(b) *Disadvantages.*

    (i) Possibility of interviewer bias.

    (ii) Little time given to respondent for considered answers.

    (iii) Surveys restricted to respondents who have telephones or, in industrial surveys, have easy access to telephones.

    (iv) Personal approach can inhibit replies.

    (v) Extensive geographical coverage may be restricted by cost considerations.

    (vi) The number of questions must usually be limited.

30. Personal interviews. These can be carried out in a highly structured way, *i.e.* the interviewer follows a rigid procedure laid down asking questions in a form and order prescribed. The interviewer may, however, be allowed varying degrees of freedom in conducting the interview. The greater the freedom allowed, the higher is the skill required in the interviewer and the more complex are the problems of analysis of the results.

(a) *Advantages.*

    (i) Greater flexibility and more opportunity to re-structure questions.

    (ii) More information can be obtained—and in greater depth.

    (iii) Resistance in respondent can often be overcome by skill of interviewer.

    (iv) Products, advertisements, etc., can be shown or demonstrated.

(*v*) Observation methods can be applied. In addition to recording verbal answers, interviewers can physically check stocks or note reactions to questions.

(*vi*) Personal data regarding respondents can be more easily obtained.

(*vii*) Sample can be controlled more effectively. Missing returns cause obvious difficulty in analysis. A skilled interviewer can arrange calls at appropriate times or make re-calls if respondents are out, or rephrase questions to which there is initially no response.

(*b*) *Disadvantages*.

(*i*) Relatively expensive if large, widely scattered geographical sample is taken.

(*ii*) Possibility of respondent bias, either to please the interviewer, to create false personal prestige image, or to end interview quickly.

(*iii*) Possibility of interviewer bias.

(*iv*) Certain types of individuals; *e.g.* important executives, people in high income groups, may be difficult to interview.

(*v*) If the sample is large and if re-calls are necessary, the time factor in completing a survey may be high.

31. The use of panels. Panels consist of *permanent samples* of the universe (*see* **18** above) and are most frequently used in consumer marketing research. Members of these panels agree to regular interviews and/or the maintenance of diaries; sometimes panel members are given small financial incentives in return for their assistance. Panels are used by company marketing research units and by marketing research agencies, *e.g.* the A. C. Nielsen company, the TAM rating system (**12** (*a*) and (*d*) above).

(*a*) *Advantages*.

(*i*) Trends in attitude, usage, etc., can be observed in easily controlled situations.

(*ii*) Panel members are obviously co-operative and usually supply very complete information.

(*iii*) Panels may be divided in order to compare reactions of different groups, for example, to products or advertisements—again under readily controlled conditions.

(*iv*) Appointments can be made, thus avoiding the expense of re-calls.

(*v*) Individual behaviour can be studied over time

periods. When different samples are taken only group trends can be examined.

(*vi*) Panel members learn instruction procedures and time may thus be saved in the future.

(*vii*) Conversations can be recorded on tape and played back.

(*b*) *Disadvantages.*

(*i*) Willingness to co-operate in a panel may indicate certain characteristics in members which are not truly representative of any particular universe.

(*ii*) If panel members drop out from time to time it is difficult to ensure that their replacements have similar characteristics.

(*iii*) There is a tendency to develop a "panel sophistication," *i.e.* constant interviewing may lead to specially conditioned responses.

(*iv*) Individual responses may be conditioned by the fact that people in groups may adapt their behaviour to what is considered to be socially acceptable.

PROBLEMS OF ACCURACY

32. Response accuracy. It is clear that, if marketing research is to provide information to guide decision-making, information must be as accurate as possible, taking into account the limitations imposed by time and cost. As we have seen, sampling itself involves a calculated risk in relation to accuracy and even in probability samples "confidence limits" are set. This means that there is a given percentage change of accuracy in the projection of the result of a sample to the complete universe. If a sample is constructed to give a confidence limit of 95% there is a 5% chance of inaccuracy. This problem is intensified by the fact that the statistical confidence limit pre-supposes that the questions posed are those to which accurate answers can and will be provided.

33. Factors in assessing accuracy of information. The following are some of the factors which must be considered in assessing the accuracy of information:

(*a*) Questions involving opinion are susceptible to greater inaccuracy than those involving fact, but even questions of fact may lead to inaccurate answers. If, for example, a physical check of stock in a store or pantry is taken, the only problems are whether the count itself is accurate and whether all stock has been seen. If, however, one asks what programme was seen on television three days earlier, the information may be inaccurate because of faulty memory or a conscious or subconscious desire on the part of the respondent to mislead. Although most respondents do not consciously try to deceive, memory can be very fallible.

(b) Respondents may not understand properly what they are being asked. The difficulty may be in the phrasing of the questions and it is wise to pre-test questions to avoid widespread misinterpretation.

(c) Respondents may not be willing to answer certain questions.

(d) The appearance or manner of the interviewer may influence the answers given. A respondent may give answers calculated to please or displease.

(e) Where questions relate to future actions, the reliability of answers depends on the extent to which people are likely to change their minds over given time periods.

(f) In posing questions on attitudes there is the problem of assessing the intensity of a favourable or unfavourable response.

(g) If questions involve the respondent in supplying reasons for an action the reasons may be inaccurate because previously they have never been consciously analysed or because they are based on false assumptions. A housewife may, for example, indicate that she buys a certain brand of tea because of its price when in fact she always buys tea at a particular shop where many brands are not available.

(h) Answers on purchasing behaviour or attitudes may be supplied by persons who make only a contribution to the decision-making process. Other members of the household or company may influence the decision to a greater or lesser extent.

(i) Buying reasons or attitudes may be subconscious and not known to the respondent.

(j) Answers may be given in order to convey a false status image, e.g. newspapers read, cultural interest.

MOTIVATION RESEARCH

34. Depth interview. The behavioural sciences, psychology, sociology, and cultural anthropology, are concerned with investigating the reasons for human behaviour. Specialists in these disciplines may undertake "depth" interviews. The term "depth" is used since the interviews are designed to discover underlying motives and desires. Depth interviews are usually undirected and require great skill and considerable time. There are difficulties not only in establishing the right degree of confidence and eliciting answers but in interpreting the qualitative information provided. This type of research is obviously expensive and, in practice, group rather than individual interviews are more commonplace.

35. Criticisms of depth interviewing. Among criticisms of the method the following are those most usually advanced:

(a) Samples are too small for meaningful conclusions.

(b) The findings are not quantified.

(c) It is difficult to know whether these investigations into the reasons for behaviour do *really* indicate a purchasing need or a motive. Attitudes revealed under research conditions may change in actual buying situations.

(d) Individual reactions in group situations are conditioned artificially by the structure and behaviour of the group.

36. Techniques in motivation research. Amongst the special techniques employed in motivation research are the following:

(a) Sentence completion tests.

(b) Word association tests.

(c) Story completion tests.

(d) Verbal projection tests in which the respondent is asked to comment on or explain what other people do; *e.g.* why do people smoke? Answers may reveal the respondent's own motivations.

(e) Pictorial techniques; *e.g.* the "thematic apperception" test in which the respondent describes what is happening in an ambiguous picture. One of the most common of these tests is the Rorschach test in which people are asked to describe what they perceive in two symmetrical ink blots. Another pictorial technique takes the form of a series of cartoons with words inserted in "balloons" above. The respondent is asked to put his own words in an empty balloon space.

37. Successful motivation research. Despite the criticisms, motivation research has been successfully applied to problems such as product design, package design, advertising, public relations, service facilities and pricing. It should also be added that some authorities maintain that valuable motivation research can be carried out by good marketing researchers who are not expert in behavioural science provided that structured questions are used and that training and direction are given by experienced psychologists.

DATA ANALYSIS

38. Preliminary care in collecting data. The care and speed of analysing data depends to a large extent on the care which has been taken in devising and executing a research project. Attention is therefore drawn to the considerations outlined in **39–41** below.

39. Constructing the questionnaire.

(a) If the survey is to be conducted by means of *structured questionnaires* to which the possible answers are predetermined, data can be readily machine-processed. Questions (and possible answers) should therefore be coded.

(b) The *length of questionnaires* should be kept to a minimum.

(c) Questions should proceed in *logical sequence*, moving from easy to more difficult questions, constantly maintaining the interest of the respondent. Personal and intimate questions should be left to the end.

(d) *Technical terms, vague generalisations* and expressions capable of different interpretations should be avoided.

40. The answers.

(a) *Replies to open-ended questions* lead to difficulties in analysis, and manual methods of analysis will have to be employed. For this reason and also because respondents and/or interviewers have to construct replies rather than simply provide an answer by means of underlining, crossing out or using a symbol such as a tick or a cross, the time allocated for the completion of the survey will need to be correspondingly greater.

(b) *Adequate space for answers* should be provided for ease of editing and tabulating.

(c) There should always be *provision for indications of uncertainty, e.g.* "don't know," "no preference."

41. Conducting the survey.

(a) Interviewers should be carefully selected, trained and briefed.

(*b*) Occasional field checks should be made to ensure that interviewers are neither cheating nor deviating from instructions. Control questions should be inserted in mailed questionnaires (*see* **28** above).

(*c*) Advance provision should be made so that appropriate action may be taken if selected respondents refuse to co-operate or are not available when an interviewer calls.

42. Editing, tabulating and analysis. When the data has been edited and tabulated, analysis can begin. The type of information required for analysis should, of course, determine to a considerable extent the manner in which the survey is planned and executed, as was indicated above (**38-41**). A careful watch should, however, be kept for *unanticipated factors* of significance.

In the process of analysis, relationships or differences supporting or conflicting with original or new hypotheses should be subjected to statistical tests of significance to determine with what validity data can be said to indicate any conclusions. For example, is it more probable that differences in the buying pattern of two groups of people as shown in survey results arise from chance selection in the sample or indicate an actual difference? (*see* Chapter XXI of W. M. Harper's *Statistics* in the M. & E. HANDBOOK Series.

MARKETING RESEARCH REPORTS

43. The content and lay-out of reports. The importance of the final report cannot be over-emphasised. This is the document which the busy executive, often unfamiliar with specialist terminology, sees and to which he looks for clearly expressed findings. The following guides to report presentation are therefore offered:

(*a*) *Lay-out.*

(*i*) All reports should carry a *title* and *date*.

(*ii*) There should be a *table of contents* so that information that the decision-maker wishes to examine closely can be located without difficulty.

(*iii*) The report should contain a *clear statement of the objective* of the research, and an explanation of the methods.

(*iv*) *A statement of findings and recommendations* in non-technical language should appear at the beginning. If findings are extensive they should be summarised.

(*v*) The main body of the report should be presented in *logical sequence* and broken down into readily absorbed and identifiable sections.

(*vi*) *Technical data, e.g.* questionnaires, sample information and statistical tables, should be put in an appendix.

(*b*) *General rules.*

(*i*) Reports should be written in a *concise and objective style*, avoiding vague expressions such as "it seems," "there may be."

(*ii*) The inclusion of *charts and illustrations* in the main body of the report should be seriously considered if they present information more clearly or forcibly.

(*iii*) *Any constraints* or calculated confidence limits should be stated.

PROGRESS TEST 3

1. What kind of questions on products or services might be answered by the use of marketing research? **(7)**

2. What are the main sources of secondary data? **(10–16)**

3. What are the main types of modified probability samples? **(20–25)**

4. What are the advantages and disadvantages of using mailed questionnaires? **(28)**

5. What are the advantages and disadvantages of personal interviews? **(30)**

6. What factors affect accuracy of replies? **(33)**

7. What techniques are used in motivation research? **(36)**

8. How should marketing research reports be presented? **(43)**

PART TWO

PRODUCT POLICY AND
THE MARKETING MIX

CHAPTER IV

PRODUCT POLICY AND PLANNING

1. Nature and scope of product policy. Product policy is concerned with defining the type, volume and timing of the products a company offers for sale. It therefore involves both existing and new products.

Decisions on products affect the following:

(a) *The company's total use of financial and manpower resources.* These resources have to be planned to meet both short-term and long-term objectives.

(b) *The kinds of customers or market areas* at which products are aimed.

(c) *The promotional methods* to be used.

(d) *The reputation* of the company.

(e) *The company's position as a leader* or follower.

THE PRODUCT MIX

2. Product lines and ranges. Few companies manufacture or handle a single item (one *line*) at a single price (one *range*). In the case of most companies there are several lines and ranges. The total assortment of products a company offers may be described as the *product mix*. In its range of assorted items a company may offer a wide variety of different items and/or a large number of quality or style variations. The product mix may be extended in various ways:

(a) By variations in models or styles.

(b) By variations in quality offered at different price levels.

(c) By the development of associated items, *e.g.* cameras and photographic accessories.

(d) By the development of completely different products in terms of customer needs, manufacturing processes, etc. ICI, for example, produces industrial chemicals, household paints and plastics among its range of products.

Product policy requires continuing attention since decisions on adding or dropping products will constantly arise. The more volatile the market, the more frequently will decisions have to be made, but the speed of change even in less volatile market areas (*e.g.* capital goods) is such that policy decisions are equally or more important since more time and more financial and manpower resources are usually required to effect change.

3. Advantages and disadvantages of multi-product operations. The greater the variety of products offered the greater, theoretically, is the market opportunity and the less the threat of complete loss of business. On the other hand, the costs of development, manufacturing and marketing may be too high to effect economics of scale, and effort may be so thinly spread that the strategic advantages of concentration are lost. Short production runs, for example, lead to high unit manufacturing costs, while advertising and selling effort scattered across a wide range of miscellaneous products and markets may be both costly and ineffective. Unless, however, as in many fields of industrial goods, there is a British or International Standard specification laid down and simplification is forced on competitive organisations, there are advantages in expanding associated lines.

Such advantages include the following:

(*a*) *Increased production of minor variations* may lead to lower unit costs resulting from a greater absorption of overhead, provided that there is sufficient increase in sales revenue.

(*b*) *Sales force costs may be reduced* if similar outlets are involved.

(*c*) *Advertising of a broad range or line* may be more effective.

(*d*) Distribution may be more readily achieved along the channels of distribution if there is a *satisfactory range in terms of consumer choice* and in terms of buying economies.

(*e*) *The opportunity of short-circuiting inefficient intermediaries* and controlling sales effort directly or closer to the end user may result.

4. The product life cycle. The sales of many products appear to follow a typical pattern, showing a gradually increasing growth to maturity, a levelling-out as saturation point is reached and then a decline. This is illustrated in the diagram which follows.

(*a*) Prior to the introduction of a product to the market there is a *development stage* during which there tends to be greater and greater investment. This investment cost must either be charged against future earnings or be written off, and it is not unnatural to find that a company which has invested large sums in a particular development project will be reluctant to abandon the research. The product life cycle concept is useful in determining the time and cost of development projects in relation to the ultimate pay-off. Frequently, large-scale development projects take much longer than originally expected and it is important to review at regular periods progress made against life cycle expectations.

FIG. 1.—The product life cycle.

(b) In the *introductory stage* costs of production and marketing will be high, but if there is a genuine product differential (an advantage not enjoyed or easily copied by other companies) a company may benefit in various ways, *e.g.* by high initial pricing or by rapid market penetration.

(c) During the *growth stage* the initial marketing efforts should lead to the greatest rate of sales expansion, but according to the rate of technical change, the rate of market acceptance, and the ease with which competitors can imitate and enter the market, buying resistance will build up. Management must therefore be ready to phase in new products and adjust marketing tactics in line with the anticipated cycle.

(d) The maturity and saturation *stages*, for example, may be the times for changes in pricing, in advertising and promotion, or in design or quality range.

(e) At the *stage of decline* profit margins become very small and every effort has to be made to reduce costs and improve distribution efficiency. Price becomes the major issue and this may, for example, lead to restriction of distribution to large outlets. A product which is at the decline stage in one country may, however, find a growth market in a country with a less highly developed economy. The cost of maintaining business at this last stage of the cycle must be weighed against the opportunity for investment elsewhere. Decline can be hastened if a company deliberately restricts production and distribution and/or pursues a vigorous policy of planned obsolescence.

5. Eliminating products. Company profit contribution frequently comes mainly from a small number of items in the product mix. Dropping products which make little or no contribution can frequently make very significant improvements in overall profitability. Weak products are very costly in ways which are not readily seen in accounting returns, *e.g.*:

(*a*) They take up a disproportionate amount of management and selling time.

(*b*) They involve short runs and high production setting-up costs.

(*c*) They often require special warehousing and transportation consideration.

(*d*) They are incurring expense which could be directed to more profitable developments.

(*e*) They may cause customers to think of the company as being unimaginative and technically unprogressive.

6. Resistance to dropping products. Frequently resistance to dropping weak products arises, for various reasons, *e.g.*:

(*a*) Management is more concerned with *new product development* than with balancing the current product mix.

(*b*) There is a *sentimental attachment* to products which were successful in the past—particularly if they were part of the original mix.

(*c*) Sales forces tend to *fear loss of individual orders* without having access to the facts of the complete marketing situation.

(*d*) *Hopes of revival* tend to linger for an inordinately long time.

(*e*) Falling sales or profits are attributed to weak *advertising or selling operations* rather than to the product.

(*f*) Dropping products may lead to the assignment of personnel to new tasks and vested interests operate to resist changes of this kind.

Products must be considered truly objectively and not continued for reasons such as these.

7. The product mix and sales growth. Companies seek to achieve profitable sales growth in the following ways:

(a) *By increasing sales of existing products in existing markets* by more efficient or more aggressive selling and promotion, or by application to new uses.

(b) *By developing improved products* for *existing* markets.

(c) *By developing new products* for *existing* markets (but *see* **8**).

(d) *By offering existing products* to *new* markets.

(e) *By offering modifications* of existing products to *new* markets.

(f) *By developing new products* for *new* markets.

8. Market segmentation and product specialisation. It should be stressed that many companies seek to develop completely new products when it might be more profitable to exploit new market segments. The economies of scale possible in capital-intensive industries, *e.g.* chemicals, draw attention to the need to exploit markets on an international scale just as much as the need to develop new product ideas. For instance, the growth in demand for paper tissue has been stimulated not only by introducing new use concepts, *e.g.* paper towels, and by extending the range in size and colour, but also by exploiting new market segments, *e.g.* industrial markets. The development of new use concepts and minor modifications may:

(a) Provide sales forces with *renewed drive.*

(b) *Stimulate distribution channels.*

(c) Build up a reputation for *progressive leadership.*

(d) *Gain free publicity.*

(e) *Secure new user market segments.*

(f) *Involve product changes at comparatively little cost.* (On the other hand, competitors may be able to imitate quickly.)

NEW PRODUCT PLANNING

9. Requirements for new product planning. New product planning involves targets and timetables for:

(a) research and engineering;

(b) plant and equipment development;

(c) commercial development;

(d) staff development;

(e) provision of financial resources.

10. Risks in new product planning. All new products involve risk, which is at its highest when the investment is high, the period of return on investment is long, and the product involves new areas of research, new manufacturing techniques and "know-how," and entry into new markets requiring new marketing skills and resources.

In order to reduce risk, the greatest possible care should be taken during the stages of *exploration, screening* and *specification*. Design testing and marketing are the really costly stages, involving many more people and greater plant and equipment resources than exploration, screening and specification.

It has been estimated that the rate of new product failure in the USA is as high as 80%. The cost of failure would probably be only one-tenth if probable failure could be detected before the design stage, by more thorough and accurate exploration and screening.

11. Sources of new product ideas. Ideas for new products can come from many sources, *e.g.*:

(*a*) from research and development personnel;
(*b*) from marketing personnel;
(*c*) from associated companies in other countries;
(*d*) from customers;
(*e*) from outside technological or scientific discoveries;
(*f*) from employee suggestions;
(*g*) from brainstorming sessions of executives;
(*h*) from competitors;
(*i*) from knowledge of government needs;
(*j*) from individual executives;
(*k*) from a study of unused patents.

12. The screening process. Screening is the process of eliminating ideas which are out of line with company objectives or resources, or which carry high risk cost and little profit opportunity (*see* **13**).

Screening and later stages of the product development process require contributions from a range of specialists, *e.g.* market researchers, engineers, development specialists, accountants. If there is no separate product planning group—and these are becoming more common—there must be detailed arrangements for *co-ordination* (*see* **31**). In technologically-based industries there is frequently too much reliance placed in the early stages on the opinions of technical specialists working in comparative isolation.

13. Screening considerations. Screening involves considerations such as the following:

(a) *Demand considerations.*

(i) What is the *potential demand* and in what markets?

(ii) What is the likely *life cycle* of the product? What is the *pattern of demand*?

(iii) What is the possibility of *substitution or product obsolescence*?

(iv) What are the *possibilities of modifying the product* to enter new market segments or lengthen its profitable existence?

(v) Will the product produce a *stable or seasonal* sales or production pattern?

(vi) What is the *maximum development time* for profit exploitation?

(vii) What are the *growth prospects* of the product in terms of the total market?

(b) *Considerations of resources.*

(i) Is the new idea in line with *company policy and objectives*, e.g. profit, image, market growth, product lines?

(ii) Is the new idea in line with *company resources, e.g.* capital, physical resources, "know-how"?

(iii) What *time, equipment and money* will be required to carry out the project and what *other opportunities* will have to be delayed or missed as a result?

(iv) Are sufficient numbers of *qualified personnel available* or can they be made available by recruitment or training?

(v) What is the *availability of materials* and bought-in components? What are the likely price variations and how will these affect final price and demand?

(vi) What *manufacturing problems* will arise?

(vii) To what extent will the product assist in *reducing production* or *marketing costs* of other products?

(viii) What will be the effect on *inventory levels*?

(ix) Can *existing distribution systems* be used?

(c) *Competitive considerations.*

(i) What *patent considerations* are involved—either the company's own or competitive patents?

(*ii*) What is the *competition*—numbers, size and resources of companies, strengths and weaknesses?

(*iii*) How do the company's likely *costs* compare with those of potential competitors?

14. Commercial evaluation. The screening process will throw up the more obvious pitfalls and opportunities which a new product offers, but desk and field market surveys will assist in defining the market or markets by size, location, structure and buying habits. Information can also be obtained on competition and other possible external factors and thus calculations can be made to indicate the share of market likely to be obtained at various time periods at various costs, and by the use of various methods of distribution, pricing and sales policies.

15. Product testing and test markets. Once the product has passed through the development and design stage full-scale production risks are avoided by building models, prototypes, or by using a pilot plant. It may also be feasible to carry out limited tests of the product in the market place. In the marketing of consumer goods a geographical area—possibly one of the smaller television areas—may be selected to test consumer and channel reaction to both product and marketing methods. A gradual extension of the test market can follow with the advantage of allowing for a gradual build-up of manufacturing capacity, inventory and selling effort.

16. Arguments for and against test marketing. The main argument against test marketing is that competitors immediately become aware of what is happening and can take steps to counter the development before national distribution or the growth stage of the product life cycle is reached.

Against this it could be argued that test markets assist in providing a realistic picture of the way in which competitors will react. The problem is to weigh the risk of failure against the advantages of a time lead—a particularly acute problem in narrowly differentiated consumer markets.

17. Operating test markets. Test markets need to be operated against controls and companies frequently use the areas on which they have previously accumulated considerable data in connection with other product launches. Competitors may, of course, react by introducing unusual variables which make interpretation of results difficult, *e.g.* running special promotions on a scale which would be uneconomical on a national basis.

Other problems arise in operating test markets, *e.g.*:

(*a*) *What should be the size and structure of the sample*—which towns, cities, rural areas, etc?

(*b*) *Over what period should a test market run* in order to obtain reliable information? What time should be allowed for initial purchase and repeat purchases, without providing invaluable cost and revenue data to competitors or incurring disproportionately heavy expenses in analysis, and production at uneconomic levels.

18. Selecting test markets. Criteria employed in the selection of test market areas have been ranked by the American journal *Sales Management* as follows:

(*a*) Typicality of distributive outlets.
(*b*) Relative isolation from other cities.
(*c*) Availability of advertising media that will co-operate.
(*d*) Diversified cross-section as to ages, religion, etc.
(*e*) Representative as to population size.
(*f*) Typicality as to *per capita* income.
(*g*) Previous good record as a test city.
(*h*) Stability of year-round sales.

19. Consumer panels. In addition to, or as alternatives to, test marketing, use is frequently made of consumer panels (*see* VII, **3**). Consumer panels are often used in an early stage of development to determine consumer attitudes or strength of preference. In industrial markets, prototypes or limited batches may be tested in the working environment on company customers or potential customers of various sizes and types.

20. Forecasting accuracy. Product testing almost always brings about changes in production methods, in design, in packaging, in pricing or in marketing procedures. A Nielsen investigation of 141 consumer products reveals that forecasting accuracy increases the longer products are on test, up to a period of 9 months. The chances of a correct projection of sales based on limited tests were as follows:

After 2 months. . . . 1 in 9
,,   4   ,, ... 1 in 7
,,   6   ,, ... 1 in 2
,,   8   ,, ... 2 in 3
,,   9   ,, ... 5 in 6

THE BREAK-EVEN CONCEPT

21. Break-even point. It is important to calculate in advance the likely relationships between cost, volume and profit over various time periods. Break-even charts are often used for this purpose. The illustration below is based on certain assumptions:

(a) That *fixed and variable costs can be separated* clearly and meaningfully.

(b) That *variable costs change* in direct proportion to output.

(c) That *price does not change* at different levels of output.

(d) That the relationships are real only at *a particular point of time.*

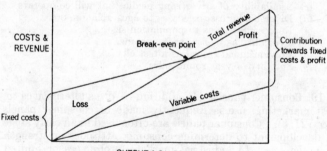

FIG. 2.—A break-even chart.

Expressed as a formula the *volume* of output at which break-even occurs

$$= \frac{\text{Total fixed costs} \quad (\text{total in £'s})}{\text{Margin of contribution} \quad (\text{£'s per unit})}$$

The margin of contribution is derived from subtracting the unit variable cost from the unit selling price.

It is often important to know the *amount of net sales revenue* at which break-even is reached on a variety of units at different selling prices. In this case, fixed costs should be divided by the margin of contribution expressed as a percentage of net sales. The margin of contribution as a percentage of net sales may be calculated from the formula:

$$1 \; - \; \frac{Total \; variable \; costs}{Net \; sales}$$

This formula derives from the fact that it is the complement of the percentage of total variable costs of net sales, *i.e.* the percentage contribution margin to net sales.

22. The effect of variable factors on break-even points and profit contributions. A decision to increase volume, apart from strategic reasons, can only be justified if additional revenue is at least equal to additional variable costs, and will provide funds for contributing to fixed costs and thus add to profits.

Break-even calculations can show the likely effect of an increase in price, or increased costs arising from the purchase of additional equipment, increased wage rates, changes in material prices, and so on. It will be clear that the higher the fixed costs the more important is the volume consideration. Capital-intensive industries are particularly susceptible to volume changes and normally demand high plant utilisation. A high investment in plant, as in certain sectors of the chemical industry, for example, may lead to a situation where home markets are insuffiently large to reach really profitable volume levels, but high plant investment and utilisation achieves the enormous economies of scale which are necessary for competitive prices in internationally competitive markets.

23. Break-even and cost concepts. Calculations of profitability depend to some extent on accounting conventions and company accounting practices. Methods of assessing costs differ considerably, as will be seen from a study of the following paragraphs (**24-26**).

24. Fixed and variable costs. *Fixed costs* theoretically remain constant over all levels of output. *Variable costs,* *e.g.* direct labour or materials, vary with changes in output level.

Fixed costs per unit of output therefore decline as production increases; variable costs per unit of output may increase if there are changes in wage rates or material prices, or decrease if, for example, materials are bought at more advantageous quantity terms. Some costs, *e.g.* power, may be partly fixed and partly variable; power for lighting may be classified as fixed, while power for operating machines may be classified as variable.

Classification into categories of fixed and variable costs depends on accounting practice and the time over which the costs are calculated.

25. Opportunity costs. In economic terms a cost incurred for any item or project means that there is a consequent loss of the opportunity to spend that money in another way.

(*a*) *Return on investment.* The cost of development of a new product involves the loss of opportunity to use resources elsewhere and consideration should therefore be given to rates of return on alternative investment opportunities. In assessing new development possibilities the following equations are useful:

$$\text{ROI} = \textit{Percentage of profit per unit of sales revenue}$$
$$\times \frac{\textit{Annual sales revenue}}{\textit{Capital invested}}$$

$$\text{ROI} = \textit{Percentage profit} \qquad \times \textit{Capital turnover}$$

(*b*) *Discounted cash flow.* Conventional accounting procedures frequently place a penalty on new developments by ignoring the fact that marketing research, technical development, tooling up, initial advertising and similar expenses are investment costs and should be treated quite differently from normal operating costs. Cost must, of course, be recovered. The problem is to establish a relevant time base and a realistic means of allocating costs directly involved in development projects.

Projects occupy differing periods of time and bring in varying flows of profit over their life cycle. One of the techniques which is being increasingly used to cope with the problem of alternative investment decisions over varying time periods is *discounted cash flow*. This technique seeks to translate future cash flows to present values by a process of *discounting*—taking into consideration the many implications of the cost of capital and the return over various time periods. Alternative investment proposals are therefore ranked qualitatively, and not purely quantitatively as in the accounting-rate-of-return method or the pay-back-period method. The notion of *opportunity cost* is involved in using discounted cash flow to decide on problems such as:

    (*i*) whether to build a new factory or expand other facilities;

    (*ii*) whether to replace existing plant by plant with higher productive capacity or rate of production;

    (*iii*) whether to lease or buy equipment;

    (*iv*) what alternative methods of financing should be adopted.

26. Incremental cost. Incremental cost is the additional total cost charge which arises from the making of a new decision. Clearly it is important to ensure that the additional cost incurred by a particular decision is more than covered by the additional revenue resulting from that decision. The concept would be particularly relevant in decisions on changes in levels of production output or in deciding whether to accept a special order at a special price. In the latter event it would be necessary to consider the likely profit resulting from acceptance as against the profit if the order were refused. Consideration would also need to be given to the possible effect on other prices in the future as well as the possible loss of alternative investment (opportunity cost).

PRODUCTS AND PACKAGING

27. Growth and importance of packaging. The growth of self-service stores and the importance of gaining distribution, shelf space and display have made packaging decisions in the field of consumer goods a highly important area of decision in regard to product policy and planning. Even in the marketing of industrial goods packaging is taking on increasing significance and extending beyond the obvious necessity of providing for production, transportation and storage.

The demand for packaging has led to an enormous increase in the range of packaging equipment and materials available. There have been spectacular increases in the use of flexible packaging involving special papers, plastics and aluminium foil. New printing methods have been developed, *e.g.* flexography, by which process it is possible relatively inexpensively to reproduce photographs or artwork in a wide range of colours on a wide range of materials.

Packaging design is influenced by the cultural, social and political environment. In the USA, for example, the housewife buys approximately 90% of her weekly purchases from supermarkets and self-service shops in one day. In the UK the percentage of food purchases from self-service outlets is much lower and there is still a great deal of daily shopping. In Latin countries pre-packed foods are rather slow in sales growth. Attitudes to colour differ; white is symbolic of mourning in many Far Eastern countries as opposed to purple in Latin countries.

28. Factors to consider in package design. A package should be designed to perform many functions:

(*a*) *Provide protection*—at any stage in the distribution process and ultimately in the home or factory of the user or consumer (*e.g.* against product damage, contamination, evaporation, chemical change, pilferage): *see* **29** below. For example, surface treatment of packaging avoids deterioration of appearance after transit and/or storage.

(*b*) *Offer convenience.* This covers handling, storage and opening of packages at all stages of distribution, and frequently in eventual use.

(*i*) *Convenience of storage in warehouse, shop and house.* In designing the package there must be a consideration of the economies of stocking large quantities of bulky, slow-moving low unit profit-margin products, and the difficulties of stacking certain carton shapes.

(*ii*) *Convenience in use.* There must be a consideration of the development of new materials and functional designs—aerosol containers, vacuum cans for vegetables, flip-top cigarette packets. New packaging ideas may lead to new products or product formulation, *e.g.* hair sprays, cheese spreads. Safety features should also be considered, as in the design of easy-opening cans eliminating the possibility of cuts and finger-nail damage.

(*c*) *Reduce transport costs.* This is achieved by the use of lightweight yet adequately strong materials, especially important when goods have to be transported by air.

(d) *Provide opportunities for re-use.* The package may be deliberately designed so that it can be used for the storage of other items once the original product is consumed, *e.g.* plastic and aluminium containers. On the other hand, some packages are designed so that refills may be bought. The design may be so differentiated that only a refill of the same product can be used in the original container.

(e) *Create a favourable product image.* The package has frequently to represent the product symbolically—to convey its buying advantages. The packaging "image" will be reinforced if there is a close tie-in with advertising and promotion (*see* VII, **21**).

(f) *Establish product differences.* The package is often the major way in which narrowly differentiated products are distinguished. The difference may be in the art design, the shape or the materials used. A package can be used to convey an impression of quality differences. Gift packs are a good example of extending the range through packaging.

(g) *Establish corporate identity.* Some companies aim at promoting individual products in their own right. Others deliberately aim at creating a company rather than product loyalty, *e.g.* Heinz baby foods.

(h) *Gain display at retail level.* The package must be easy to arrange on shelves or racks and at the same time should attract the potential customer. Developments in printing techniques, *e.g.* flexography (*see* **27** above), combined with newer packaging materials, *e.g.* polyethylene film, have significance in this connection.

29. Packaging and protection. In considering some of the more sophisticated uses of packaging the protective aspects of packaging should not be disregarded. Attention is therefore drawn to the following hazards against which packaging should provide a defence:

(a) *Damage by mechanical handling.* Most damage occurs in the handling process and, the more frequently products are handled in the distribution process, the greater is the need for protection. One of the advantages of the liner train and other container transport development is that they will result in less damage through handling. Damaged goods have to be replaced and are likely to cause loss and inconvenience to seller and purchaser. Often slightly damaged products may not be returned, but may inhibit repeat purchase.

(b) *Product loss.* Liquids and powders are highly susceptible to loss, *e.g.* powder leakage, liquid evaporation.

C

(c) *Pilferage.* Loss through pilferage can be quite high—especially if there are many handling points.

(d) *Contamination by dust or dirt.* Clothing, food and fine machinery are obvious examples of products liable to damage in this way.

(e) *Moisture gain and loss.* Many products have an optimum moisture content, *e.g.* cement, ceramic paints, frozen foods.

(f) *Chemical change, e.g.* metal corrosion, coffee rancidity.

(g) *Flavour loss or change.*

(h) *Mould, e.g.* in canned foods, paints.

(i) *Insect attack, e.g.* moths in clothing.

ORGANISATION FOR PRODUCT PLANNING

30. Principles of product planning organisation. It is dangerous to generalise on ideal organisational arrangements for product planning since companies differ in so many ways. There are, however, certain important principles which should be observed:

(a) Product policy depends greatly on the attitude of top management and it is vital that top management should be constantly alive to change in the market.

(b) If product planning is to be consumer oriented, marketing personnel should be closely involved from the earliest stages of development and throughout the life cycle of the product.

(c) Product planning involves the co-operation and co-ordination of specialists with different attitudes—engineers, scientists, accountants, marketing men, production specialists. It is necessary, therefore, to set up clear definitions of responsibility and authority in relation to product decisions and to ensure that there are easy and known systems of communication (*see* VIII, 1).

31. Co-ordination through groups. One of the problems of organisation for product planning is to ensure that vested interests do not dominate or produce conflicts. There will, in fact, often be a strong case for establishing a new *product-planning group, as well as product managers* responsible for co-ordination of activities and profitability of existing products or product groups. The product planning group may consist of a committee of executives which meets at regular intervals or a permanant "staff" group freed from the problems of day-to-day line operations. The completely separate "staff" group is most commonly found in large organisations and is normally concerned with new product development. Existing products are, in these cases, under the direction of product or product group managers, reporting in turn to the senior marketing executive. When new product planning is carried out by an independent group it is important that a mechanism exists for decision-making, so that new products can be moved over to line product managers at the appropriate time.

32. Use of networks in product planning. One of the ways in which the various actions necessary by different people at different times can be effectively co-ordinated is by the use of network analysis. A network is a graphical representation of a project showing all activities linked sequentially in such a way that interdependencies are clearly seen, *i.e.* when the beginning of one activity depends on the completion of other activities. Timings are shown so that it is possible to see the earliest and latest times at which an activity can begin. The shortest possible time for completion of the project can also be traced along the network. This is the *critical path*, any delay along which will cause a hold-up in the completion of the total project. Cost elements can also be built in, if desirable, as well as a range of alternative time estimates.

33. Decision tree. Another technique which may be used in product planning is the *decision tree*. It has been made clear that product planning involves a sequential decision-making process and that at various stages a decision to stop the project or to follow an alternative course of action could be taken. The decision tree is based on the notion of probability. At each decision point an estimate is made of the probability of success or failure and the consequent effect on loss or gain. In Fig. **3** (taken from a paper by J. F. Magge in the *Harvard Business Review*) a decision tree is used to show the likely outcome of alternative investment decisions.

34. Cost, revenue and price. Determination of product policy and planning the most profitable product mix are

highly important and complex areas of management. Cost
and revenue considerations have to be calculated and estimated
as precisely as possible. The effect of price on costs and
revenue will be examined in the next chapter.

FIG. 3.—Decision tree.

PROGRESS TEST 4

1. What are the advantages and disadvantages of multi-
product operations?   (3)

2. What is meant by the "product life cycle"?   (4)

3. Why is there resistance to dropping products?   (6)

4. What are the main considerations in screening ideas for new
products?   (13)

5. What criteria might be used in selecting test markets?   (18).

6. Construct a break-even chart.   (21)

7. What is meant by (a) "opportunity costs"; (b) "incremental
costs"?   (25, 26)

8. Why is more attention now being paid to packaging?   (27)

9. How might networks be used in product planning?   (32)

10. What is a decision tree?   (33)

CHAPTER V

PRICING AND DEMAND

PROBLEMS OF PRICING

1. Perfect competition. A great deal has been written by economists on the interaction of price and demand. Much of this writing was based on a situation in which price was the dominant variable differentiating products or services. *Perfect competition* demands that goods from different producers are identical, that there are identical circumstances under which a sale takes place, that complete information on products and markets is equally available to all potential buyers, and that there are sufficient producers to prevent restriction of supply to one (monopoly) or a limited few (oligopoly) producers. Such conditions hardly ever exist and the growth of an affluent society has further complicated the quantitative assessment of elasticity, *i.e.* the sensitivity of demand in relation to price.

2. Imperfect competition. More recently it has been realised that in a society where everyone is living above mere subsistence and exercising discretionary spending power, with ever wider ranges of goods available from competing producers, qualitative variables take on an increasing importance. *Imperfect* markets and *imperfect* competition are a feature of a sophisticated capitalist or mixed economy. This is not to deny the existence of varying degrees of demand elasticity. Economic pricing theory has relevance to practical marketing situations. The more a product or general product category is regarded as a necessity the more inelastic is demand likely to be. If discretionary incomes fall, the demand for food will continue whereas the demand for washing machines will decline. Likewise the demand for exotic expensive foods will decline much more than the demand for bread. Again, with all products there is an upper and a lower price level, outside which demand would fluctuate sharply; the problem is to determine those levels. Within a given price range some products have a more elastic demand pattern than others, but too little is known of these more subtle elasticities since there is a tendency for competitors to follow each others' pricing systems fairly closely in order to avoid the risk of the unknown. Demand is a measure of the utility that a product has for a consumer or a market and price is only one aspect of that utility.

3. Factors of demand. Factors which may affect demand can be subsumed under three broad headings:

    (a) Market considerations (*see* **4**).
    (b) Company and product considerations (*see* **5**).
    (c) The demand for other products (*see* **6**).

4. Market considerations. Demand is affected by the size of the market and the needs and desires of the people constituting that market.

    (a) *Population.* Total population in most parts of the world is growing and the size of markets is increasing. On the other hand, populations are becoming more mobile and even industrial concentrations are shifting—sometimes as a result of government economic policy. Demand for both goods and services will, therefore, depend to some extent on the direction of marketing effort to particular market sectors.

    (b) *Disposable income.* A highly developed industrial society has a large proportion of the population with considerable discretionary incomes. Countries in early stages of development have fewer people above subsistence level but there may be a small layer of society with exceedingly high levels of disposable income. Government economic policy and especially taxation systems may affect actual and anticipated disposable income levels very considerably. Expectation of earnings or profits has a marked effect on demand for deferrable items, *e.g.* luxury goods, plant and equipment.

    (c) *Customer satisfaction.* People are motivated to buy goods and services for a whole host of economic, social and psychological reasons. Current fashion, individual taste, prestige, imitation of others, the relative importance of comfort, convenience or security, may all have a bearing on buying behaviour. Some products may even sell better in certain markets because they are higher in price.

5. Company and product considerations. Demand for a

product is obviously influenced by the ideas people have about that product and the company that manufactures it.

(a) *Company or product reputation.* The higher the price range of the product, the more it is likely to affect health or security, or the more influence it may have on the performance of other products, the more is a purchaser likely to avoid untried commodities from little-known firms.

(b) *Advertising and promotion.* A product must be known before it is bought. Selling skill or the creation of a favourable product image through advertising may have a very considerable effect on purchasing action. "Promotional elasticity" is a measure of the changes in demand relative to advertising expenditure.

(c) *Service.* The provision of pre- or post-sales advice and servicing facilities may more than compensate for an initially high price.

6. The demand for other products. The following factors are important.

(a) *Cross-elasticity.* The demand for goods may be influenced by the demand for other goods, which may vary according to price.

(b) *Competition.* Demand will depend not only on the price of competitive products or substitutes but on their reputation, availability, performance, aesthetic appeal, length of service, flexibility of use and so on.

(c) *Derived demand and choice.* The demand for almost all products is conditioned by the demand for others. Sometimes the buying problem is a question of deciding on the use of limited resources to buy one make of car as opposed to another— or to go on an overseas holiday instead of buying a car. Sometimes there is a close dependency in the demand for one product on the demand for another. The demand for nylon depends on the demand for nylon-finished products. The demand for machines depends on the demand for the goods the machines produce. It is sometimes possible for the manufacture of derived demand goods to stimulate primary demand; *e.g.* the promotional campaigns of manufacturers of fabrics in man-made fibres led to an increased demand for the fibres and for the raw materials and machinery.

7. The problem of changing variables. The problem of pricing is intensified not simply because of the increasing *number* of variables affecting demand, but also because those

variables are in a *constant state of change*. It is a basic task of
marketing to determine which of the variable factors of demand have greatest significance in particular markets at particular points of time. Attempts to determine the factors at
present range from sheer guesswork or intuition to the construction of complex mathematical models. Successful product differentiation depends on the determination of the
relevant factors and the creation of some of the elements of
monopoly benefits.

8. Specific price problems. These can be summarised thus:

(*a*) To establish a price structure in markets where there is
known to be wide pricing latitude.

(*b*) To set a pricing structure for new products.

(*c*) To change existing price structures.

(*d*) To decide on action to counter change in competitors'
prices.

(*c*) To establish prices for products with inter-related costs
or market demand.

BASIC PRICING POLICIES

The majority of companies have no clear pricing policies.
Where these do exist they usually follow one or more of the
principles outlined in the following paragraphs.

9. Market penetration. Low prices are set in order to
penetrate markets, to gain a major market share—usually
in a comparatively short time. This policy can only be valid
if the market is very price-sensitive, and/or if production
costs fall significantly in line with volume increase, and/or if
competitors will be discouraged. If penetration targets are
achieved and competitive activity has been restricted, the
problem of whether to raise prices or reduce margins to
intermediaries, *e.g.* wholesalers, retailers, might arise.

10. Short-term profit maximisation. A policy of setting
very high prices in order to make as much profit as possible
in a short time is normally only valid if the producer has an
innovation of such significance that there is a ready price-
elastic market with virtually no immediate competition but

likely competition in the near future. The producer must also normally be prepared to move out of the business when he has made his quick profits. The Reynolds International Pen Company introduced ball-point pens at a retail price of $12·50 and in three months made a profit after taxes of $1,558,608 on an investment of $26,000. Competitive pressure forced prices down and the company closed, but the originator made a fortune. A primary objective of most companies, however, is to stay in business.

Short-term profit maximising (or "skimming the cream") pricing objectives have sometimes been applied successfully to segment markets, to recover costs quickly in conditions of uncertainty, or to compensate for high development costs. Books are often produced first in a limited expensive edition and, in the light of demand indications, cheaper paper-back editions may follow. New drugs are often extremely expensive initially but prices fall rapidly after the first one or two years of the product life.

11. Satisfactory rate of return. Some companies fix their prices on the basis of a traditional rate of return over a given time period, related to the extent of risk or investment involved. In its most sophisticated form this becomes *target pricing*. Target pricing is aimed at securing in a given period of time a pre-determined rate of return on investment. The process involves the calculation of an average mark-up on average costs and at the same time projecting sales revenue at various stages of the product life cycle. Target pricing is thus directed towards the twin objectives of stabilising prices and yet achieving a given return on investment over the product life. At particular points of time the return will be high; at others low.

Target pricing demands accurate forecasting and accurate costing in terms of levels of output and marketing expenditure. Problems lie in the fact that, despite the importance of other factors, price remains a factor of demand, and this method ignores the influence of different price levels on volume.

12. Product line pricing. Many companies selling a wide range of products gear pricing to a range of products rather than to individual products. It may be considered that certain products yielding a comparatively low profitable return

are necessary to support products which yield a high profit.
At the extreme some products may even be "loss leaders"—
products which are basically non-profitable or just over
cost—which stimulate buying of other profitable lines. "Loss
leaders" are a feature of large retailing operations; *e.g.* a
housewife who buys low-priced aspirin tablets may be tempted
to buy at the same time a perfume carrying a high profit.

13. Cost-plus pricing. This pricing method guarantees
that no product is sold at a loss since a fixed percentage or
mark-up is added to costs. It takes little or no account of
subleties of demand analysis. Cost-plus policies are often
used by retail traders and in manufacturing industries where
there is non-standardised production.

The fact that retailers or wholesalers may operate traditional
mark-up policies must be considered by manufacturers in
organising the pricing structures. Fairly narrow standard
ranges of mark-up have become commonplace for particular
commodities and manufacturers' price policies demanding
change need most careful planning. The problem is
intensified by the fact that retailing costs are less susceptible
to change than manufacturing costs; *e.g.* increases in material
prices and variations in the volume of throughput of goods
affect the costs of manufacturers more than those of retailers.
Cost-plus pricing is also frequently based on data accumulated
as a result of past experience.

Attention should also be drawn to the following:

(*a*) *Variations in margins.* Cost-plus pricing varies according
to the nature of costs to which the margins are added. Examples
of these variations are as follows:

(*i*) *A margin is added to direct production costs* to cover
costs of distribution, overhead and profit.

(*ii*) *A margin is added to direct production and distribution
costs* to cover overhead and profit.

(*iii*) *Differential overheads* (an estimate of the overhead
costs incurred as a result of taking on the particular business)
are allocated to total product or product group costs and the
added margin covers profit only.

(*b*) *Variations in costing.* Cost is an important factor in
price determination yet there are great differences in both cost
concepts and costing practice. *Overhead allocation* is a major
problem area. Some processes, *e.g.* in the chemical and oil

industries, result in automatic production of a range of products. Oil-refining leads inevitably to production of petrol, kerosene, asphalt, heating oil, to name but a few. Allocation of joint costs in line with volume would be nonsensical in terms of the prices which the markets will bear. Should the market price determine the cost allocation, or should by-products escape production cost charges altogether? Major international companies have not yet resolved these problems satisfactorily.

Once cost is known, what *cost base* should be used for pricing, *e.g.* full cost, incremental cost, marginal cost, opportunity cost, past or future cost, short-term or long-term cost, variable or constant cost?

NOTE.

   (*i*) Full cost is based on average total cost of each unit of output plus a margin for profit.

   (*ii*) Incremental cost is the additional variable cost associated with an additional unit of output.

   (*iii*) Marginal cost is the additional total cost per unit associated with an additional output volume.

   (*iv*) Product costs are recorded only for items or activities which vary directly with the volume of output, *e.g.* direct material, direct labour, variable factory overhead.

14. Variable pricing. This is most commonly applied to products or services with known variable time demands. It may be used to take advantage of extra profit at peak periods or to reduce production and overhead costs by stimulating demand in non-peak periods. Hotel rates may be high in peak holiday seasons and low in winter and autumn. Specially reduced rates for use of electricity at off-peak periods may be introduced to utilise output more effectively and even cut the production load.

Occasionally differential pricing may be negotiated with individual customers, though this is a risky practice, or disproportionately high profit margins may be demanded for unusual extras, such as a television set with a particular type of wooden cabinet or a car with special chrome fittings.

15. Competitive-based pricing. Most companies set prices after careful consideration of competitive price structure. Deliberate policies may be formulated to sell above, below or generally in line with competition. One of the problems here is that cost and profit structures and practice will differ.

The more closely a company's price policy is geared to match or undercut competitive prices, the more important it is to bring cost into line, to accept a lower rate of return or to provide a product package which is really different.

Many companies attempt to keep price levels in line with an average rate for the industry (the "going rate"). The "going rate" is a valid policy where market conditions are highly competitive and where products are narrowly differentiated. This is a major problem of commodity and raw material trading, upon which many under-developed countries depend so much.

Close competitive pricing is also found in markets where one company or a small group of companies is in a highly dominant position and can either directly or indirectly regulate prices of materials or components used by small price-cutting organisations, or stand the strain of a price war much more readily. In some cases one company clearly emerges as a price leader.

16. Bid pricing. When contracts are awarded as a result of tender, *e.g.* government contracts and large-scale plant construction, companies must clearly attempt to determine the level of competitive bids. If the object is to obtain the contract, cost will be considered mainly to determine the minimum price level. Calculations of anticipated profit against probability of tender price acceptance may be undertaken. In some cases mathematical models have been constructed, but in the last resort the problem of discovering what prices competitors will bid remains.

DISCOUNTS

Discounts involve the offer of reductions (differentials) from a base price and must also be considered when price policy is being determined. The following are the most usual forms:

17. Trade discounts. In areas where there is resale price maintenance (R.P.M.), such as in some parts of the USA, the fixed retail price is usually the base. Elsewhere, as now in the UK, a suggested or expected retail selling price might be used. Prices to retailers might be at list price less a percentage discount to cover the retailer's margin. Prices to wholesalers might be at list price, less retail discount, less a discount to cover the wholesaler's margin. Although, except in R.P.M. conditions, there is no control over resale prices, discounts have some stabilising influence on final prices.

18. Quantity discounts. Price advantages might be offered on the basis of order size or particular assortments.

Quantity discounts might be applied to retailers and wholesalers within their own prices structure, or there may be a general quantity rate pricing structure which gives bulk-buying advantages to retailers and wholesalers equally—size of business or order being the only criterion.

Quantity discounts may attract large buyers or induce smaller buyers to order large quantities. Most quantity discount arrangements apply to either single orders or single deliveries and these involve economies of scale in transportation and administration. Some discounts are paid retrospectively on the basis of orders received or goods delivered. In some countries there are legal restrictions on discount procedures, *e.g.* in the USA.

19. Cash discounts. Most business transactions from manufacturer to wholesaler and/or retailer are conducted on credit terms. The length of time allowed for payment varies considerably and payment in practice is often delayed beyond the duration of the officially stated credit terms. When this happens the supplier has the problem of deciding how rigidly to press for payment, and whether to refuse to supply further goods. Some suppliers offer a special discount for payment within a stipulated period from the date of invoice.

20. Seasonal discounts. These may be offered to stimulate sales at special times of the year or day, *e.g.* "off-peak"-period railway tickets.

21. Geographical differentials. These are differential rates offered in relation to distance from supply base, *e.g.* petrol zone pricing, new car delivery.

NOTE: Transportation charges may be designated F.O.B. factory or warehouse. Transport costs are then added to net prices quoted.

PRICE CHANGE AND CUSTOMER ATTITUDES

22. Problems of price-changing. The risks involved in price change either upwards or downwards are so great that suppliers are usually slow to act. They are particularly slow to move prices upwards, knowing that such action will affect competitors, ultimate buyers, intermediaries, and will also be subject to government scrutiny. The fact that prices of particular types of products. tend to move upwards or downwards at a particular time may be the result of:

(*a*) Unofficial inter-company communications.

(*b*) Changes in cost factors which affect all suppliers, *e.g.* variations in material costs, new wage agreements.

(*c*) A fear of loss of business if prices are not competitive.

(*d*) Action which should have been taken previously but has been delayed in order to avoid placing the company in an isolated pricing situation.

23. Estimating reaction to price changes. Some of the methods of pre-judging reaction are as follows:

(*a*) *Attitude surveys*: field interviews based on statistical samples.

(*b*) *The use of mathematical models* constructed from significant and controllable socio-economic variable factors.

(*c*) *Statistical estimates* based on regression analysis and simple or multiple correlation (*see* **24** below).

(*d*) *Experimental pricing* in limited test markets.

(*e*) *The use of operations research techniques*, such as game theory, to anticipate likely competitive reaction (*see* **25** below).

24. Regression and correlation analysis. Regression analysis is a statistical method of examining the past trends of relationships between one variable, *e.g.* sales volume, and one or more than one other variable, *e.g.* advertising expenditure, cost of salesmen. Correlation analysis is a statistical method by which it is possible to measure the closeness of those relationships. Regression analysis will show that there is a relationship between disposable personal income and the sales of most consumer goods. Correlation analysis will show how close that relationship is in the case of specific consumer items. When an increase in one variable coincides with an increase in another, the two variables have a positive correlation. When an increase in one coincides with a decrease in the other, the variables have a negative correlation. The highest possible correlation is expressed at + or − 1. Simple correlation is restricted to the relationship between two variables. Multiple correlation takes into account the simultaneous relationship of more than two variables.

25. The use of operations research techniques. Operations research is a comparatively new science derived from many disciplines, *e.g.* mathematics, physics, engineering, economics. A basic concept is the building of a model, usually mathematical *i.e.* sets of equations relating significant variables in a situation to the outcome. Professor Stone of Cambridge has constructed a model of the economy, for example, in an effort to study and forecast the effect of changes of variables, *e.g.* Gross National Product, on the whole economy and on other variables.

Operations research is essentially designed to assist in resolving complex problems and after being developed in the 1940s to tackle military problems it is now being applied increasingly to business situations. One of the many techniques is *game theory*, by which it is possible to examine systematically the possible reactions by a competitor or competitors to a company's change in strategy, *e.g.* increasing or decreasing price to wholesalers.

The probabilities can be estimated and decisions assisted by knowing in advance the likely outcome ("pay-off").

26. Psychological factors. Price reductions may not be immediately accepted as inducements to purchase for the following reasons:

(*a*) There may be a suspicion of *lower quality*.

(*b*) It may be thought a product is *faulty* or comparatively unacceptable and, therefore, has to be at a reduced price.

(*c*) Experienced buyers may anticipate *further reductions* and wait until they judge prices have reached their lowest level.

(*d*) It could be imagined that there was a *danger of obso-*

lescence. Price reductions sometimes precede the entry of new models.

(e) Buyers—especially industrial buyers—*may prefer maximum price stability* as an indication of reliable trading practice. Frequent price changes may give an impression of financial instability.

(f) Many purchasers—particularly domestic consumers— are *unaware of the precise price* of a wide range of goods and only become aware if there is a change, when they tend to re-assess the values of competing products.

(g) Customers may not have a precise knowledge of prices of existing products but they usually have *firm ideas of upper and lower* limits or a "price zone." Prices outside the zone may have to overcome additional psychological barriers. The price zones for new products are much more vague and there is little or no opportunity to compare. This greater pricing latitude for new products is not always utilised by manufacturers.

(h) *Some people like to be innovators* or to be seen as innovators; others follow. Price attitudes of leaders and followers may be quite different.

(i) Price notions may be geared to the *coinage system.* Elementary use of this idea, such as 19s. 11d. instead of £1, is still sometimes effective (and such practices may continue when decimal coinage is introduced), but there may be other price barriers associated with coinage which we know little about.

However, early price values do persist and, provided there is *quality acceptance,* reduced prices may be seen as bargains.

PRICING TACTICS AND DEMAND

27. Pricing and research and development costs. Frequently companies set prices for new products with the objective of recovering research and development costs in a given time period. Research costs do not necessarily relate to individual product success and an attempt to recover disproportionately high research and development costs by high pricing may indeed reduce profit by inhibiting demand.

There is much to be said for covering the costs of research and development by aiming at the highest revenue above marginal cost. Consumers will not pay for research as such, but for the *distinctive utility*—economic, psychological or social—which the product offers. In the last resort, products should be measured by the contribution they make to overhead and profit. Working in reverse and basing prices on arbitrary allocation of general overheads, whether they be management, research or clerical administration, can never be justified except perhaps for a "one-off" guaranteed sale.

28. Indirect pricing differentials. Non-listed special allowances, service provision and other concessions are sometimes used (to major customers) in non-differentiated product markets. Other indirect concessions may take the form of margin guarantees, special credit terms and allowances to wholesaler, retailer or agency advertising or promotional campaigns.

Indirect price competition is openly seen in many consumer markets in offers of various kinds, *e.g.* the use of coupons for free trials or for purchases at reduced prices. There are, for example, banded packs with two similar products at a special price, premium offers of gifts on purchase, and "trade-in" concessions for durable items. These special offers to domestic consumers may be supported by special deals to channel intermediaries. Some offers are described as self-liquidating, *e.g.* goods supplied at bargain prices in return for tokens indicating product purchase. Theoretically the "bargains" are achieved by the manufacturer obtaining goods at bulk prices and passing on the advantages to individual customers.

29. Reasons for special promotions. In general, however, special promotions represent a temporary price cut and are used for various reasons:

(a) *Novelty appeal.* It is claimed that permanent price cuts are easily imitated and it is difficult to return to the original prices. Promotions on the other hand have a novelty appeal and can be a way of differentiating one product from another.

(b) *Psychological advantage.* Promotions, it is said, have a psychological advantage in creating a greater impression of extra value than a price cut.

(c) *New customers.* A special offer may be the means of persuading people to try a product for the first time and some of the business gained will be retained when prices are normal; loyal customers also gain the advantages of the temporary price cuts.

(d) *Opportunities for selling.* Promotions in highly competitive consumer markets provide salesmen with a series of new presentations and an opportunity for acquiring shelf space. These promotions are almost invariably supported by display materials.

(e) *Uneven demand.* Promotions may help to smooth out uneven demand.

In general promotions are more frequent at the launching of a new product campaign.

30. Pack size and price. It is sometimes difficult for a customer to compare prices of similar products since there is often a wide range of pack size and differences in the weight of the contents. Although it may be necessary legally for the manufacturer to stipulate on a carton the weight of the contents the purchaser may completely disregard weight-price comparison, or be unable to make the comparison, *e.g.* between grammes and cc. The increase in pre-packed consumer goods has made direct price comparison much more difficult. Frequently virtual price increases are disguised by decreasing the size of the pack, *e.g.* in confectionery.

31. Competitive pricing and company policy. Pricing policy, as has been seen, is related intuitively or by calculation, to cost, demand and/or competition. Companies should, therefore, study not only their own costs but also likely competitive cost structure. If competitors change prices it will be necessary to decide on a line of action. The more products are seen to be similar, the more likely it is that prices will move in line. On the other hand, there have been examples of a company's maintaining prices when competitive prices move up and yet successfully improving market share or profits.

If products are differentiated a company must consider what part price plays in the total marketing mix. After determining why a competitor has reduced price, for example, it will be necessary to estimate whether the price change is likely to be permanent and what the likely outcomes of various reactions might be. Competitive price cuts could be met by temporary indirect offers or a change in packaging, or an increase in advertising and sales effort. The timing of reaction will be important. It may be essential in some market situations to adjust prices immediately—in others there will be an opportunity to wait.

255,
25/0/0
1.

Mrs. Correia

Mrs E. D. Aguiar
105 Rowena Drive Apt #320
Don Mills
Ontario Canada

Mrs H. Dahn
27 Wagner Drive
West Hill
Ontario Canada

Mrs P. Prince
6 Northfield Road
Scarborough
Ontario Canada

Mr J. Valladares
79 Packno Blvd
Scarborough
Ontario Canada M1R4J8

Miss Nadia Khomi
105 Rowena Drive Apt #414
Don Mills
Ontario Canada

32. Conclusion. Pricing is a key marketing decision area. Doing nothing, provided this is a deliberate decision, is a policy. Successful pricing decisions will always be the result of a combination of art and science, but it is increasingly possible to measure the probabilities of the effect of external forces in the environment in which a company operates. More certainly it is possible to devise pricing policies which meet company objectives. No longer should a company be in the position of effecting a hasty compromise between conflicting objectives in complete ignorance of the likely market response.

PROGRESS TEST 5

1. What are the major factors influencing demand? **(3–6)**
2. What is meant by "penetration" pricing and "product line" pricing? **(9, 12)**
3. To what extent do companies set prices in line with those of competitors? **(15)**
4. What are the main types of discount? **(17–21)**
5. In what ways can the effects of price changes be estimated? **(23)**
6. What psychological factors influence the attitudes of buyers to price? **(26)**
7. What are the reasons for special promotions? **(29)**

CHAPTER VI

ADVERTISING AND PROMOTION: OBJECTIVES AND INSTITUTIONS

THE PURPOSE OF ADVERTISING

1. Definition. Advertising is an impersonal form of communication aimed essentially at persuading customers and potential customers—including middle-men along various channels of distribution—to adopt a favourable attitude to an identified organisation, product or service.

2. Campaign objectives. Examples of campaign objectives are as follows:

(a) To inform potential customers of a new product or service.
(b) To indicate new uses of an existing product.
(c) To remind customers of an existing product in order to maintain loyalty against competing pressures.
(d) To give information about desirable qualities of a product.
(e) To stimulate enquiries.
(f) To give reasons why wholesalers and retailers should stock a product.
(g) To provide technical information about a product.
(h) To build a corporate company image.
(i) To give information on price changes, special offers, etc.
(j) To explain available technical services.

3. Advertising and profit contribution. As advertising is one of a number of variable elements of marketing strategy, operating in a constantly shifting market environment, it is virtually impossible, except in mail-order selling or certain direct mail campaigns, to quantify exactly its contribution to profits. The more precise the objectives are, however, the easier it is to estimate the value of a campaign and to design an effective campaign.

4. The sales task approach. When sales tasks can be closely defined, *e.g.* to increase product awareness amongst decision-makers in a given percentage of a market during a predetermined number of months, or to expand dealer stock levels by a certain percentage over a given time period, it is possible not only to direct campaigns specifically towards the achievement of stated tasks, but also to assess the contribution advertising is likely to make towards the accomplishment of those tasks.

5. Advertising and the sales process. It has been said that the sales process consists of six basic steps, *viz*:

(a) making contact;
(b) arousing interest;
(c) creating preference;
(d) making a specific proposal;
(e) closing the sale;
(f) retaining business.

It is possible to assess the contribution which can most effectively be made by advertising towards the achievement of one or more stated objectives at each of the six stages. The justifiable cost of achieving the contribution by means of advertising can then be assessed in relation to total marketing expense. Consideration can also be given to the cost of alternative means of communications, *e.g.* employing extra salesmen. In this way a more realistic measurement of the economic level of advertising expenditure can frequently be made.

ADVERTISING AND THE MARKETING MIX CONCEPT

6. Factors influencing buying decisions. The sales-task approach to fixing and measuring the effectiveness of advertising expenditure is not always possible, and when it is used it is clear that the probability assessments of the contribution that advertising can make towards the attainment of objectives must rely on judgment as well as on facts. Apart from the problems involved in estimating the external changing market forces affecting sales (*e.g.* competitive activity, economic climate, customer attitudes, trade attitudes and government controls) a marketing organisation has to take into account the wide range of forces it can bring to bear in order to influence buying decisions. A potential customer may be influenced to a greater or lesser extent by any combination of the following:

- (a) Performance of the product.
- (b) Aesthetic design features.
- (c) Packaging.
- (d) Service facilities available.
- (e) Advertising.
- (f) Promotions which give temporary special incentives to buy.
- (g) Personal calling.
- (h) Channels of distribution.
- (i) Margins allowed to dealers along the distribution channels.
- (j) Distinctiveness of the product, e.g. branding, quality.
- (k) Price to the ultimate buyer.
- (l) Credit facilities.
- (m) Store display.
- (n) Convenience of handling in transportation, warehousing or end use.

7. The marketing mix. The complex of marketing decisions which may stimulate sales is frequently called "the marketing mix"—a term originally used by Professor Neil Borden of the Harvard Business School. The marketing mix may be seen to consist of elements concerned with the product, e.g. range, price, quality, with channels of distribution, and with communications. Communications involve the whole process of communication with markets, e.g. advertising, personal selling, public relations. The sales-task approach to fixing and measuring the effectiveness of advertising expenditure depends on an understanding of the various possibilities of combinations of elements in the marketing mix. The basic elements of the marketing mix for machine tools may be products of rigid quality-control standards, high unit prices, low advertising expenditure, high personal selling cost, direct distribution from manufacturer to user. In contrast, the basic marketing mix for flour may involve greater product quality variation, low unit price, comparatively high advertising expenditure with low personal selling cost and indirect distribution through wholesalers and retailers.

8. Advertising expenditures. Advertising expenditures in relation to total marketing costs (costs of physical distribution and promotion as opposed to production costs) vary very widely. Sometimes they may be as high as 40% or 50%; sometimes as low as $\frac{1}{2}$%. In general, the percentage of advertising expenditure is a greater proportion of marketing costs in the case of consumer than of industrial goods and services. Regularly repeatable consumer products with mass distribution objectives, such as soap and chocolates, are particularly heavily advertised.

Too frequently there is a completely subjective estimate of advertising expenditure. Marketing research, costing studies and operations research can increasingly assist in determining the appropriate budget to be allocated to advertising and promotion elements of the marketing mix.

Some of the attacks made on high levels of advertising expenditure take no account of the cost frequently incurred in other elements of the marketing mix. In the 1966 Monopolies Commission investigations, evidence was provided to show, for example, that, while detergent advertising and promotions accounted for 16% of marketing costs as opposed to 6% in the case of ice cream, trade margins for detergents were restricted to 19%, while they were as high as 32% for ice-cream. The strategies of individual companies marketing similar products may differ considerably. The report on advertising compiled by the Confederation of British Industry in 1967 draws attention to an average of 15% of sales spent on advertising by US cosmetic companies as against 2·7% expended by the Avon Company. Avon, however, rely on personal selling with correspondingly higher costs in sales incentive payments.

9. Pull and push strategies. When greater reliance is placed on the personal selling efforts of a company's sales force or of distributor salesmen than on advertising, an organisation may be said to the pursuing a "push" strategy. A "push" strategy is typical of the marketing of industrial machinery, for example. Where it is not possible to bring strong direct selling pressure to bear on the end customer a "pull" strategy may be used. Manufacturers selling grocery products, for example, usually feel that there is inadequate personal selling effort directed by wholesalers and retailers and great attention is paid to advertising and promotion which "pull" the product along the channels of the distribution and into the hands of the ultimate buyer. Push and pull strategies are therefore related to the types of products being marketed, and also to the external forces bearing on markets and company policies at particular time periods.

ADVERTISING AND THE PUBLIC INTEREST

10. Criticism of advertising. The Confederation of British Industry's report mentioned above draws attention to the two major areas of criticism against advertising, *i.e.*:

(*a*) Advertising is wasteful.
(*b*) In certain circumstances heavy advertising by a dominant supplier may restrict competition by preventing new entrants to its markets.

11. Economic justification of advertising. The Confederation of British Industry's answer to the first charge (**10** (*a*)) is basically that successful companies must be profit-minded and organise their expenditure in a way calculated to obtain the best return. From a company point of view advertising may be justified when the increase in revenue is greater than the cost of advertising provided that this is the most satis-factory—and profitable—of the various possible uses of scarce resources. Companies will examine expenditure parti-cularly carefully because:

(*a*) profits are being squeezed, since costs are tending to rise proportionately faster than revenue;
(*b*) demand patterns are changing more rapidly;
(*c*) high levels of investment are put at risk.

12. Advertising and the danger of monopoly. The second point of criticism (**10** (**b**)) implies that by means of advertising a company can create such a consumer loyalty that it can build up the level of its sales to a scale where advertising becomes a very small proportion of individual unit costs; the resulting economies of scale will provide the opportunity for pricing flexibility along the distribution chain. This pricing flexibility, it is argued, could be used to prevent the entry of competition not having advantages of large-scale production and distribution. This goal achieved, prices could be raised to a level of unethical exploitation of the consumer. A monopoly, or oligopoly, operating contrary to the public interest could thus be created.

This second criticism is based on the premise that companies lack ethical standards, a premise which could be argued at length. The larger and more successful a company becomes, the more its policies are under public scrutiny and business ethics are no longer a matter of academic discussion; they are the vital concern of boardrooms.

Accepting, however, a lack of ethical considerations, the criticism rests upon *the mistaken notion that products and markets do not change*. Examples of companies who have been able to enter fields dominated by more powerful organisations by providing products having demonstrable technological or economic advantages are not difficult to find. Wilkinson's inroads into the razor-blade market against the powerful Gillette; Lloyd's Automotives' break through into the car-care field against giants such as Johnsons, Simoniz and Howards; Lesney Products' rise from a two-man firm in 1947 to a leading international die-cast toy organisation—these are just three examples of outstanding success in the marketing of consumer goods where advertising is normally reckoned to be such a large factor in the marketing mix. It might be argued that new entrants in fields where products are more narrowly differentiated are more difficult to find, *e.g.* petrol, chocolate, cigarettes, but in the case of petrol there is also the important barrier of very high capital investment costs, while chocolate prices in the UK are lower than anywhere in Europe.

13. Public benefit from advertising. An argument in support of advertising and the public interest which is often ignored is that by advertising a supplier is identifying his company or his company's products. This attempt to create a distinction must be accompanied, if it is to be successful, by the setting of quality standards. Research has shown that, while it is sometimes possible to find that the price of certain strongly advertised products may be higher than those of a random selection of non-advertised goods, the variation in quality of the advertised products is much less than that of the non-advertised products. Advertising, therefore, would appear to reduce the risk to the consumer of buying low-quality products.

CONTROL OF ADVERTISING

Advertising is subject to restrictions in various media, imposed by both internal and external bodies. Some of these voluntary and statutory controls are outlined in **14–18** below.

14. The British code of advertising practice. This code is accepted by all organisations operating advertising media— press, television, cinema, posters, direct mail. The code was first published in 1962 and revisions are made from time to time, but many voluntary control systems had been applied long before that. The *Molony Committee on Consumer Protection* in its 1962 report gave support to the principle of *voluntary control* embodied in the Code.

(a) *Member organisations.* These include:

(i) the Advertising Association;
(ii) the British Poster Advertising Association;
(iii) the Independent Television Companies Association;
(iv) the Institute of Practitioners in Advertising;
(v) the Screen Advertising Association;
(vi) the Newspaper Proprietors' Association;
(vii) the Newspaper Society.

(b) *Basis of the code.* No advertisements contravening the Code may be accepted for publication (*see* **15**). The Code covers such matters as:

(i) public decency;
(ii) exploitation of superstition;
(iii) appeals to fear;
(iv) misleading descriptions and claims, including scientific terms, testimonials, price, guarantees, disparagement, imitations, medicines, mail order, advertisements addressed to children.

15. The Advertising Standards Authority. This body was established as a limited company in 1962 and is independent of the advertising industry, although it is financed by the Advertising Association. Members are appointed as individuals and not as representatives of an organisation or special group interest. There are a chairman and ten members—five connected with advertising and five entirely independent of advertising interests. The Authority, in addition to keeping in touch with the Committee responsible for the control and revision of the Code, adjudicates on general advertising issues and special disputes amongst advertising bodies. It deals with complaints from the public and investigates action or non-action on reported breaches of the Code. For example, the Consumer Council complaints of alleged misdemeanors in advertising are reported to the Authority.

16. Statutory controls. There are many Acts of Parliament restricting or controlling particular aspects of advertising. Students should refer to a specialised text, such as *Modern Advertising Law* by Peter Langdon-Davies (Business Publications Ltd. on behalf of the Institute of Practitioners in Advertising, 1963), for a more detailed treatment. Examples of statutes affecting advertising are:

Sale of Goods Act, 1893.
Merchandise Marks Act, 1887–1953.
Indecent Advertisements Act, 1889.
Cancer Act, 1939.
Pharmacy and Medicine Act, 1941.
Television Act, 1954.
Food and Drugs Act, 1955.
Copyright Act, 1956.
Obscene Publications Act, 1959.
Betting and Gaming Act, 1960.
Town and Country Planning, 1947, and the *Town and Country Planning (Control of Advertisements) Regulations*, 1960.
Civil Aviation (Licensing) Act, 1960.
Hire Purchase Acts of 1938, 1954 and 1957.
Noise Abatement Act, 1960.
Labelling of Food Order, 1953, and later amendments.
Pre-Packed Food (Weights and Measures). Marking Regulations, 1957.
Trade Descriptions Act, 1968. This extends the provisions of the *Merchandise Marks Acts* and provides for enforcement. The Board of Trade may make orders defining terms when used as part of the trade description of goods, or require

specified information to be given with goods or in advertising
for goods.   Services are also included in this type of legisla-
tion for the first time.   False or misleading indications of
prices are prohibited.

17. The Television Act, 1954.   One Act only—the *Television
Act* of 1954—attempted to establish a control of advertising
in such a way that advertisements are inspected before they
are shown to the public.   The Independent Television
Authority (I.T.A.) set up by that Act has the statutory power
to inspect every advertisement before it is transmitted.   Such
a rigid control exists in other media only in the case of medical
products (where the Proprietory Medicines Association of
Great Britain has set up a voluntary control system to which
all members subscribe).   Television programme contractors
may screen only advertisements which have been passed by
the I.T.A.

The I.T.A. has established its own "Code of Advertising
Standards and Practice" with full legal backing and has an
Advertising Advisory Committee consisting of representatives
from the advertising industry, the general public, the Ministry
of Health, the British Dental Association and the British
Medical Association.   The composition of the Advisory
Committee indicates clearly the emphasis given to protection
of the public in the case of false or misleading claims in
connection with products affecting physical health.   Some
of the major problems concern areas where is is difficult—
if not impossible—to set down meaningful rules.   The I.T.A.
is to exclude, for example, anything which "offends against
good taste or decency"—but is it possible to legislate on
"good taste"?   As the Confederation of British Industry's
report (8) suggests, in the end much depends "on the subjective
judgment of individual people and on their collective sense
of public responsibility."

18. Other codes and standards.   Individual organisations
within the advertising industry endeavour to control advertising standards by setting their own very specific regulations
for membership or for accepting advertisements.   Amongst
these are:

(a) The "Bye-Laws Relating to the Standards of Practice"
of the Institute of Practitioners in Advertising.

(b) "Regulations covering the Acceptance of Advertisements for Display," issued by British Transport Advertising Ltd.

(c) "Standards of Practice Regulating Contracts for Localised Advertising," drawn up by the Advertising Association.

(d) "Form of Application by an Advertising Agency," for recognition by the Newspaper Proprietors' Association Ltd. and the Newspaper Society.

(e) "Standard Conditions of Insertion of Advertisements," in newspapers in membership of the Newspaper Proprietors' Association.

(f) "Standard Conditions of Trading," laid down by the British Poster Advertising Association and the London Poster Advertising Association Ltd.

(g) "Advertising Film Standard Conditions," agreed by the Screen Advertising Association and the Institute of Practitioners in Advertising.

(h) "Standard Conditions observed by Producer House Members," of the British Direct Mail Advertising Association.

ADVERTISING AGENCIES

19. What are advertising agencies? Advertising agencies are specialists in the planning, creating and placing of advertising. They function, therefore, between the advertiser and the media owners. An agency may assist in suggesting product features or sources of ideas. It may be asked to design trademarks and packaging, to advise on selling and promotional policy and to plan advertising campaigns. It will have artists and copywriters for creative work or will arrange for this to be done. Agencies prepare advertising schedules of media to be used and reserve and pay for the space or time (*see* 22 and 23 below).

20. Numbers and business transacted. There are over 500 advertising agencies in the UK with great variations in size of business transacted (billings), numbers employed, and range of services offered. Almost all national advertisers (over 25,000) use advertising agencies, even though they may have their own advertising departments. Many regional and local advertisers—and there are probably as many as 40,000 of these—use agencies to some extent. Some 90% of all expenditure on advertising media passes through agency hands. More than half of the agencies are members of the Institute of Practitioners in Advertising and these account for some 90% of total agency business.

21. I.P.A. conditions. Conditions of membership of the I.P.A. by an agency are that:

(*a*) It is equipped to provide the kind and type of advertising service and marketing advice to which the advertiser is entitled.

(*b*) Its personnel includes fellows and/or members of the Institute.

(*c*) It promises to observe the Institute's standards of practice.

(*d*) It is free from any vested interest in advertising media or facilities.

(*e*) It will avoid advertisements of an undesirable, unethical or offensive nature.

(*f*) It will not canvass accounts of fellow members unless at the written invitation of the advertiser.

(*g*) It will not submit speculative advertisement designs or copy to any but its own clients except on payment of an adequate fee and only after an exhaustive study of a client's problems at first hand.

22. Agency remuneration. Agencies receive from the media owners a commission ranging from 10% to 15% on time or space booked. As agencies are involved in providing marketing research, marketing and campaign plans and other services it is sometimes necessary for them to fix a minimum charge for small accounts or to ask for a special service charge. Many specialist trade and professional papers allow only 10% commission and this fact, together with the comparatively low level of advertising expenditure of companies using these publications, frequently leads to agencies specialising in mass consumer goods campaigns. The agency accepts credit responsibility for its client as far as the media are concerned and media owners have, therefore, no legal right of action against an advertiser in the case of default. Agencies must, therefore, be investigated and recognised as financially sound by official media owners' organisations.

23. Creativity and campaign planners. There is a growing tendency for agencies to become involved in total marketing strategy and it is sometimes suggested that, as a result, the really major work of an agency—creativity—suffers. There is certainly considerable evidence that a great deal of advertising is dull and unimaginative. Potential customers are becoming subjected to more and more advertising and there is a need for freshness of impact if campaigns are to be effective. The constant repetition of badly conceived advertising may well create buying resistance. On the other hand, it is obviously necessary for agencies to understand an advertiser's corporate strategy and marketing objectives, and close working relationships should exist.

24. Agency personnel. The agency link man is the *account executive* who works with the brand manager or appropriate company advertising executive. The account executive calls upon agency or outside experts in organising the campaign in line with the advertiser's objectives. The agency, therefore, employs or engages the temporary services of specialists in copy writing, creative art, typography, printing, television and film production, as required. It has staff who specialise in, advise on and plan the use of various media, in addition to those who actually buy space or time. Larger agencies have ancillary services such as marketing research departments which may undertake tasks such as testing advertising impact or providing information necessary for campaign strategy. The large agency with high billings can afford to carry specialist staff which even the largest advertiser would find difficult to justify economically, and the constant employment of that staff—often on related products in similar markets—can provide a wealth of experience on which to draw. Conversely, it could be argued that frequently repeated narrow experience can lead to creative sterility.

Agency organisations differ enormously and so do the needs of advertisers. An advertiser with a large marketing department of its own is unlikely to require the same kind of strategic advice which is required by an advertiser with a small marketing staff.

PROGRESS TEST 6

1. Give examples of advertising campaign objectives. (2)
2. What is meant by the "sales task" approach to advertising? (4)

3. What is the difference between "pull" and "push" strategies? **(9)**

4. Is advertising against the public interest? **(10–13)**

5. What are the main provisions of the British Code of Advertising Practice? **(14)**

6. In what way is the *Television Act* of 1954 unique in the matter of advertising control? **(17)**

7. What are advertising agencies and how are they paid? **(19–22)**

CHAPTER VII

ADVERTISING AND PROMOTION: CAMPAIGN PLANNING AND EVALUATION

BASIC STEPS IN CAMPAIGN PLANNING

1. The five basic steps. There are five really basic steps in the process as follows:

   (a) Objective (*see* VI, 2).
   (b) Copy.
   (c) Media.
   (d) Marketing co-ordination.
   (e) Budget.

These are outlined in **2–6** below.

2. Determine the objective of the campaign. This is a task for company management (*see* VI, **1–7** above) and not for the advertising specialist who may, however, cause management objectives to be modified if it is felt they cannot be achieved because of copy, media, budget or other limitations.

3. Decide on the advertising copy. Copy may clearly depend on choice of media, and this and the next step will often be considered together. An early examination of copy is necessary since the whole process of advertising is based on the ability to communicate a message to an audience which should, as a result, react favourably to the product or service. In general, the most effective copy is that which concentrates on a limited selling appeal and frequent repetition of a single appeal is a feature of many very successful campaigns. Certainly many campaigns are spoiled by the attempt to cover too many selling points in one advertisement. Campaigns may, of course, be planned to cover a number of single objectives over a given time, in line with a multiple communications strategy: *i.e.* to inform potential users of the company's technical achievements; to inform intermediaries in channels of distribution of a new product; to inform users of technical service offered with new product.

Advertising can be pre-tested to determine whether the intended message is being communicated and comparisons of the effectiveness of communication of a number of advertisements can also be made. Samples of prospective viewers or readers are exposed to advertisements and certain reactions are measured. Sometimes, tests are carried out on specially constituted panels. The tests may be conducted on the basis of aided or unaided recall of advertisements to which the panel or sample member has been exposed. It should be noted that these tests relate to the effectiveness of the communication as such and do not give a measure of sales results (*see* **9–11** below).

4. Select and schedule appropriate media. Problems of media selection include the following:

(*a*) The extent of coverage required to reach potential buyers and the effective cost of reaching them.

(*b*) The comparative communication effectiveness of various media, *e.g.* the compatibility of the advertising or editorial material (*see* XI, **7, 15**) with media audiences. An advertisement designed for the popular press might be totally unsuitable in a learned journal.

(*c*) The administrative, organisational and operating requirements of the media, *e.g.* operating frequency of publication and length of lead time required for placing advertisements.

(*d*) Consideration of the ways in which competitors allocate expenditure to various media.

(*e*) The determination of advertising frequency—"opportunities to view."

(*f*) The size, positioning and/or timing of advertisements.

5. Co-ordinate advertising with the total promotional plan. Amongst co-ordination problems would be those of assigning tasks and expenditure to point of sale display, personal selling efforts, dealer support programmes, handling and follow-up of enquiries, special promotional activity such as premium offers, contests, etc.

6. Determine and control the advertising budget. The size of the budget will, in practice, determine very largely the selection of media, but ideally budgets should be determined by companies after due consideration of the cost of achieving communication objectives.

EVALUATION AND RESEARCH

7. Advertising contribution and research. Basically management needs to know what contribution advertising makes to sales and profits. The complexity of the marketing mix makes precise evaluation extremely difficult. The sales task method which is based on value judgment of the likely contribution of advertising (*see* VI, **4, 5**) is gaining ground, but most attempts at evaluation are investigations into specific aspects of advertising in isolation.

8. Target audiences and media data. The type of information readily available to advertisers is improving but is still very limited in both quantity and quality. It can be classified as follows:

(*a*) *Data on circulation or viewing, e.g.* the circulation of newspapers and magazines, the number of people passing poster sites, the number of television sets switched on to commercial stations at given times of the day.

(*b*) *Data on total audiences, e.g.* information on the number of readers of a single copy of a newspaper or viewers of a television programme.

(*c*) *Data on audience characteristics, e.g.* analysis of readership by social, geographical, economic groupings.

(*d*) *Data gained from specific studies* carried out by media owners on, for example incomes, spending patterns, buying habits, product usage of readers or viewers (*see* III, **14**).

9. Media research. This is aimed mainly at:

(*a*) analysis of the *actual size of audiences* or readership of print media at particular times; and

(*b*) analysis of *attitudes* towards advertising messages.

Probability samples may be used and data may be collected be electronic devices, *e.g.* the television measurement system (*see* III, **12** (*d*) above). Most research is, however, undertaken at periods of time after advertisements have been seen. Postal questionnaires and personal interviewing are employed. Selected respondents are sometimes asked to maintain diaries. Researchers may use "aided recall" techniques which imply that memory is stimulated in some way, *e.g.* by showing a list of programmes and inviting identification of those seen or heard. None of this research gives a measurement of the *sales effectiveness* of advertising.

10. Copy research. This is aimed at assessing the differences in impact of various sizes, themes, lay-outs, visuals, colours, etc. Research may be carried out both before and after the appearances of an advertisement. The tests used include the following:

(a) *Advertisement mock-ups*, shown to consumer juries who are asked to indicate preference, usually by ranking scales or by paired comparisons. The latter method involves a statistical calculation of the number of pairs possible from a given number of trial advertisements. (Paired comparisons are also frequently used for testing reaction to new products.)

(b) *Eye movement analysis*, using cameras to trace not only the direction of eye movement but also the length of time spent on particular parts of an advertisement.

(c) *Readability studies*, aimed at assessing communication ease and effectiveness. These studies may include research into the understanding and emotional impacts of words by people of different standards of education and from different cultural backgrounds as well as studies of word and sentence length, etc.

(d) *The use of electronic equipment* to record favourable and unfavourable responses to advertisements.

(e) The *Schwerin test* is a method of assessing the effectiveness of advertisements in influencing consumers to buy the product. In a theatre situation an invited audience is exposed to TV or press advertisements. Before and after exposure the audience is asked to place a number of brands in the order in which they would most like to win them as a prize in a lottery. Change or shifts in preference are then assumed to measure the effect of the advertisement on the audience.

(f) *Recognition and recall tests*. These tests are widely carried out by personal interview (usually on the basis of a standard questionnaire); they vary mainly in the extent and method of memory stimulation.

(g) *Analysis of enquiries received* from advertisements specifically designed to elicit requests for further information. In mail order selling and where salesmen can follow up enquiries it is possible to establish an order conversion rate. The conversion rate may, however, depend very largely on marketing factors such as price or special product features.

11. Image research. An increasing number of studies are being made to discover what buyers—whether industrial, wholesale, retail or domestic—think about products and companies. Well-planned attitude studies may lead to changes in the total marketing strategy, and often to redirected emphasis toward company or product image building. There is a growing use of psychologists to undertake this type of research by individual or group discussion methods.

12. Test markets. (*See* IV, **17, 18**). The effectiveness of particular campaigns is frequently judged by setting up control and test areas so that, against other known criteria, differences in sales results may be observed. The problems of establishing controls and measuring a range of possibilities, within time constraints imposed by competitive reaction, are obviously very great. The decision to buy is, however, conditioned by price, product design, personal selling efforts, advertising, promotions, user recommendations, availability, display, packaging—marketing forces within the control of the seller—as well as by forces outside the seller's control. A buyer must become aware of the existence of a product or service, understand its benefits, become convinced of the desirability of those benefits and take buying action. Ranged against the buying decision are such forces as competition, sales resistance, memory lapse and alternative use of available resources. This complex of variables makes the establishment of research controls to measure the impact of advertising exceedingly difficult and progress during the next decade will depend on four main developments:

(*a*) Clear definition of *advertising goals* as part of the total communications and marketing goals (see VI, 2).

(*b*) More definition of *target audiences*.

(*c*) Greater use of *behavioural science* concepts (*see* III, **34**).

(*d*) The application of *multi-variate statistical techniques, e.g.* factor analysis, with faster, more complex experimental analysis made possible by use of computers. Multi-variate techniques are necessary to examine relationships between sets of variables, *e.g.* attitudes on first purchase and second purchase, and advertising copy and frequency.

MEDIA AND COSTS

13. Advertising media and expenditure. The major advertising media in the UK may be broken down as follows:

(*a*) National newspapers.

(*b*) Regional newspapers.
(*c*) Magazines.
(*d*) Trade and technical press.
(*e*) Television.
(*f*) Cinema.
(*g*) Radio.
(*h*) Outdoor media, *e.g.* posters, transport, wrapping paper.

Total expenditure on advertising was estimated at £590 million p.a. (2·6% of consumers' expenditure) in 1965. There is every reason to believe that there has been an overall increase since 1965 of some 5%, which would bring the figure to over £600 million. Note that these figures do not include expenditure on classified advertisements for jobs, sales promotion, political and government department campaigns. Sales promotions, such as catalogues, gift schemes, exhibitions, window and store displays, account for approximately £120 millions.

14. Circulation, viewing figures and media cost. Spending on television advertising has grown to such proportions that television advertising expenditure now runs slightly ahead of national press advertising expenditure. Women's magazines represent the next most popular medium. Statistics prepared by Legion Information Services Ltd. show the level of press advertising in April 1968 at £158·4 million (a decline of 2·2% against the April 1967 level) with television advertising at £129·3 million (an increase of 7·7% in the corresponding period). Costs of space or time are fairly closely linked to circulation or viewing figures. The cost of a half page in the *Daily Express* is considerably more expensive in absolute terms than the cost of similar space in *The Times*, while the cost of advertising at peak viewing times in the Midlands would be considerably greater than that of advertising at peak viewing times in the Tyne-Tees area. There are some economies of scale for large-scale advertisers in special rates and discounts as well as the less easily quantifiable advantages of cumulative impact.

If a target audience is, however, defined in terms of class groups the effective costs of various media may be completely different. The socio-economic classes generally accepted at present are as follows:

A.	3%	⎫
B.	10%	⎬ upper
C.1.	17%	and
C.2.	38%	middle
D.	28%	⎫ working
E.	4%	⎭ and poor

Thus consideration must be given to the fact that, while some 51% of readers of *The Times* are considered to belong to classes A and B, only 33% of the *Daily Express* readers are in these catagories. On the other hand the *Daily Express* claims some 40% of the C.2 class amongst its readership as opposed to 17% in the case of *The Times*.

15. Other factors in assessing "effective cost." Many other factors enter into the calculations of the "effective cost" of media, *e.g.*:

(*a*) Circulation and viewing figures vary geographically, as do buying patterns. Television, for instance, is transmitted on a regional basis. It is therefore possible to direct advertising to specific geographical areas and this situation is frequently used to provide test market information.

(*b*) Television has a greater attention-pulling potential, especially if demonstration is needed, but social class coverage can be achieved on a more selective basis by use of press media.

(*c*) A single newspaper advertisement may be seen more than once by the same person. Sunday and weekly papers in particular are retained longer and provide additional opportunities to view. An I.P.A. readership survey indicates that 3·5 readers see each individual copy of women's magazines.

(*d*) It has been estimated that some 80% of consumer purchases are influenced by women. Regional press has an average housewife readership of some 83%. Sixteen million women over the age of 16 read magazines—some 79% of all women in the country. *Woman*, for example, has the highest circulation amongst women of any magazine in the world. There is also some evidence that women's magazine readers are younger, more prosperous, more beauty and fashion conscious and more progressive than non-readers. The extensive use of colour in these magazines is another advantage.

(*e*) Two-thirds of the current cinema audiences consist of young adults (16–34 years of age). Attendance by people between the ages of 21 and 24—largely engaged or newly married couples—is as high as three times every four weeks.

Size of press advertisements, length of television commercials, intensity of readership or viewership, frequency of insertion or transmission and spread of expenditure amongst viewer media, are all important variables to be considered in calculating advertising effectiveness in relation to cost.

Furthermore, it should be remembered that decisions to buy a product or service are sometimes the result of formal and informal discussion amongst several people often with different interests and attitudes. (This is particularly true of industrial markets.) In addition, buying attitudes and spending patterns of individuals in similar socio-economic groups vary.

MEDIA SELECTION AND MATHEMATICAL MODELS

16. An advertising cost/effect model formulation. Attempts are being made to create mathematical models (*see* III, **20**(*c*)) to determine the relationship between advertising costs and effectiveness. An early basic equation evolved by the Americans Vidale and Wolfe is:

$$\frac{dS}{dt} = rA\frac{M - S}{M} - \lambda S,$$

where S = rate of sales at time t,

$\dfrac{dS}{dt}$ = increase in rate of sales at time t,

A = rate of advertising expenditure at time t,

r = sales response constant (sales generated per advertising dollar when $S = 0$),

M = saturation level of sales,

λ = sales decay constant (sales lost when $A = 0$).

17. Difficulties in building advertising models. Major difficulties in model building are as follows:

(*a*) *The delayed sales impact* of a great deal of advertising. Advertising may often be regarded as a form of capital budgeting.

(*b*) *The importance of quality* as opposed to quantity. Creativity in content and in presentation is a highly significant feature of many of the most successful campaigns.

18. Media selection models. The most promising development in the use of models have taken place in media selection (a detailed example is given in Chapter 12 of of G. B. Giles' *Case Studies in Marketing*, Macdonald and Evans).Optimising methods, such as linear programming, are being used to arrive at media selection yielding maximum exposure subject to given constraints, *e.g.* a set advertising budget, maximum use of certain media, a minimum target audience exposure rate. Optimising is the process of allocating scarce resources in such a way that an objective is reached in the most effective way. Linear programming is a mathematical technique which can be used if the relationships between the variable resources can be expressed by linear equation. The computerised model is only an aid to judgment with the great advantages of speed.

Amongst the problems are the following:

(*a*) Omission of or judgment quantification of qualitative factors.

(*b*) Lack of precise knowledge of the effect of the timing and frequency pattern of advertisements.

(*c*) Lack of precise knowledge of the effect of the overlapping of readership amongst various media.

(*d*) Changes in the interest value of editorial or programme material—a very marked problem in television advertising. An advertisement appearing alongside a press report of an international soccer match or immediately after the presentation of a sporting event on television would have a different effect from one appearing by the side of an article or after a programme with an essentially feminine appeal.

ADVERTISING BUDGETS

19. Methods of determining advertising budgets. Some of the most common methods of determining advertising budgets are as follows:

(*a*) *As a percentage of sales.* "Sales" may relate to overall turnover, or to revenue received for individual products or groups of products. Some companies work on current sales figures; others on projected sales.

(*b*) *On the basis of competitive advertising expenditure.* While competitive advertising must be considered, no two companies are pursuing identical objectives from an identical base line of resources, market standing, or other factors. Determination of budgets on the basis of, say, an identical percentage of gross sales revenue to that of competition is completely unrealistic.

(c) Both as a percentage of sales and in relation to competitive advertising expenditure.

(d) As the amount remaining after deduction of other expense plus a predetermined return on capital. This method appears to be based on the premise that it is impossible to determine the optimum level of advertising but that it is right to advertise success to almost any level. Major objections lie in *(i)* the short-term emphasis which may lead to problems in longer-term advertising investment needs; and *(ii)* the lack of consideration of alternative investment opportunities.

(e) As a cost of achieving a given objective. This is the most logical approach, but the difficulties of setting objectives and measuring their attainment have been previously discussed *(see* VI, **3–5**). This method may serve to determine the minimum and maximum limits, but there will usually be a considerable margin between these two. Objectives have also to be taken not only in relation to cost, but in relation to their contribution to profits.

Many companies apply information which has been developed through budgetary control systems indicating profitability of markets, types of customers, products, etc. Problems remain in that a great deal of marketing expense is arbitrarily allocated and there is great need for improvement of cost accounting practice applied to marketing.

If the "objective" approach is used, however, the cost will be considered against other budgetary considerations, *e.g.* the total budget for promotion, for marketing and for the business as a whole. If budgets have to be reduced, it is vital to reconsider the advertising objectives.

BRANDING

20. Brand identity. A feature of advertising policy—particularly in the case of consumer goods—is to establish a brand identity. A brand identity may begin with a name, *e.g.* "Kleenex", "Tide," but extends to other visual features—typography, colour, package design, slogans—features which should assist in creating, stimulating and maintaining demand. It is clear that branding could have a contrary effect if either the branded product were unacceptable to the consumer or the branding image were psychologically or sociologically ill-conceived.

21. Reasons for branding individual products. Amongst arguments in favour of branding are the following:

(*a*) Memory recall is facilitated. This could lead to more rapid initial buying action or greater frequency of buying and, hence, deeper loyalty.

(*b*) Advertising can be directed more effectively and linked with other communications programmes.

(*c*) Branding leads to a more ready acceptance of a product by wholesalers and retailers.

(*d*) Self-selection is facilitated—a very important consideration in self-service stores.

(*e*) Display space is more easily obtained and special promotions are more practicable.

(*f*) The importance of price differentials may be diminished.

(*g*) Brand loyalty may give a manufacturer greater control over marketing strategy and channels of distribution.

(*h*) Other products may be introduced more readily. (The failure of a brand may, of course, lead to undue resistance to other products.)

(*i*) The amount of personal persuasive selling effort may be reduced.

(*j*) Branding makes market segmentation easier. Different brands of similar products may be developed to meet specific categories of users.

The relevance of branding does not apply equally to all products. The cost of brand advertising and promotion may be prohibitive. Again, the success of branding may depend both on the nature of the product and on the behaviour characteristics of customers. Branding, for example, demands the ability to control quality; it is also likely to be more successful where product attributes are difficult to evaluate objectively. To take extremes, it is obviously easier to brand whisky than iron ore.

22. Corporate images: advantages and disadvantages. Instead of branding individual products, companies sometimes create product family images or a corporate company image associated with all products. The potential cost saving of the approach is clear but certain problems arise. These include the following:

(*a*) Difficulties of marketing different quality grades.

(*b*) Difficulties of marketing a range of products which it may be undesirable to relate closely.

(*c*) The risk of damage to existing lines by the introduction of unsuccessful products.

(d) The difficulties of devising sufficiently clear advertising and communications objectives and assigning expenditure. Companies which pursue an individual brand policy normally have brand managers who are concerned with the marketing and profitability of particular brands, and responsibility accounting methods can therefore be employed.

23. Private branding and quality control. In recent years wholesaling and retailing organisations which do not manufacture have been promoting their own brands—products supplied by manufacturing organisations with special labels and packaging. The most successful operation has been carried out by Marks and Spencer, who lay down precise specifications and exercise rigid quality control over manufacturers who supply "St Michael" products. Multiple food stores are, however, increasingly involved in the branding battle—frequently without the resources to specify or control quality.

24. Reasons for the development of private brands. The major reasons for this wholesaler and retailer action are as follows:

(a) A desire to limit the control exercised by manufacturers of strongly branded products.

(b) A desire to create a company or store identity and, hence, loyalty.

(c) A desire to introduce greater price variation. Private brands are frequently cheaper.

(d) A desire to protect margins. Intensive competition amongst powerful manufacturers sometimes leads to low retail and wholesale margins.

Small manufacturers are not unnaturally attracted by what appear to be easy markets, but larger manufacturers also frequently supply private brands, both to achieve given production levels and thus absorb fixed costs, and to take defensive action by accepting business which might otherwise go to a competitor and strengthen his costing structure or trade goodwill.

PACKAGING

25. Uses of packaging. Packaging may be considered from three basis standpoints:

(a) as a protective device;
(b) as a product utility factor; and
(c) as a form of promotion.

These were discussed earlier in IV, 27–29. Packaging is, however, a sufficiently important element in promotional communication to justify its discussion again at this point.

26. Communication and package design. The advent of self-service has created a packaging revolution. The package on the store shelf and in the housewife's pantry is a form of advertising which is attracting increasing design attention— design to be linked with other forms of advertising. A brand name on a package which cannot be reproduced effectively on television, for example, is useless to the detergent manufacturer. When buying depends to a great extent on impulse, package shape or colour may be the major means of creating product preference. Ideally consideration of product design should include:

(a) Ease of identification in all selling situations, *e.g.* set against competitive products on store shelves.
(b) Appeal both in shop and in household. Contrast the likely household location of soap powders and paper tissues; packaging should appear suitable for its likely location, as well as being attractive in itself.
(c) Ability of cartons or outers to be quickly converted into display units.
(d) The impact of product visibility, *e.g.* use of glass containers, visi-packs, etc.
(e) The impact of colour and the problems of reproduction in other media.
(f) The pros and cons of returnable and non-returnable packaging.
(g) Differences in national and sometimes regional attitudes and behaviour.

27. Packaging technology. Increased attention to packaging has led to a growing use of industrial designers as well as packaging technologists. Packaging costs are rising and although the main impact of the packaging revolution has been seen mainly in the field of consumer goods its marketing potential cannot be ignored by industrial goods producers— particularly those who are tackling international markets.

Packaging exhibitions in Tokyo, Copenhagen, Milan, Dussel-
dorf, Paris and Moscow have attracted much more than casual
interest.

The growing cost, complexity and time required to develop
package designs point to a greater need for top management
co-ordination and direction of packaging policy as a vital
factor in achieving sales.

SPECIAL SALES PROMOTIONS

28. Consumer promotions. Special sales promotions are
part of indirect advertising programmes intended to stimulate
quick action. They are a- feature of packaged consumer
goods selling tactics and are directed at the consumer and/or
the trade. The following are examples of consumer promotion:

- (a) Special price sales.
- (b) Free sample distribution.
- (c) Premium offers.
- (d) Contests.
- (e) Point of sale demonstrations.
- (f) Coupon offers.
- (g) Combination or banded-pack product offers.

29. Trade promotions. The following are examples of
trade deals:

- (a) Provision of display materials.
- (b) Co-operative advertising schemes—assistance with blocks
  or space costs.
- (c) Contests for sales staff.
- (d) Special discounts.
- (e) Special quantity rate terms.

30. Reasons for special sales promotions. Special promotions are almost invariably used at the time of launching a
new consumer product to gain maximum dealer stocking,
display space and customer attention. Costs vary from the
high expense of free sample distribution to "self-redeeming"
premium offers where goods bought at special quantity terms
are supplied at bargain prices to customers who return coupons
or other evidence of purchase. There are so many special
promotions in the more highly competitive areas of consumer
marketing that it would be dangerous for a company not to be

involved.   Other reasons for the use of special sales promotions
include the following:

    (a) Stimulating a new use for a product.

    (b) Encouraging more frequent use of a product.

    (c) Appealing to a special segment of the market.

    (d) Boosting sales in particular geographical areas.

    (e) Encouraging the use of another product (combination
        offers).

    (f) Attracting bargain-hunting non-brand-conscious buyers.

    (g) Encouraging seasonal sales or stimulating off-peak period
        sales.

    (h) Creating dealer interest and encouraging stocking.

    (i) Securing shelf space.

    (j) Encouraging movement of slow-selling lines.

    (k) Offsetting price competition.

    (l) Assisting sales force presentations.

31. Display.   The importance of display in consumer
selling cannot be overemphasised.   Manufacturers may have
special display posters, stands, cards and other material
designed for windows, counters, shelves, floors.   Many
manufacturers' salesmen are trained to set up displays and
in new food lines there is an increase of "rack jobbing"—a
jobber taking over responsibility for stock and display, with the
retailer providing space at a somewhat lower profit margin.

32. Trading stamps.   The use of trading stamps as a form
of sales promotion developed rapidly in the late 1950s.   For
some five years the Green Shield Trading Stamp Company
had little competition but the American Sperry and Hutchinson
Company appeared on the British scene in 1963.   This form
of promotion is financed by the retailer at a cost of some
$2\frac{1}{2}\%$ of turnover.   There has been considerable argument
about the effect of stamps on customer prices.   There is
some American evidence to indicate that prices in stores
using trading stamps tend to increase by the cost of the stamps.
To profit from the use of trading stamps without raising
prices clearly means that gross revenue must be expanded.
Nevertheless, many retail outlets are clearly deriving advantages from stamp trading, but competition is increasing and
it is not uncommon to find double or treble stamp issues on
certain commodities or on particular days of the week.

33. Publicity. Publicity may be defined as news about products or companies appearing in the form of editorial material, without cost to the sponsor, in the press, on radio, television, stage, etc. "Without cost" refers to space or time costs, since good publicity programmes depend on the skill of publicity specialists. Activities range from recipes appearing with brand names in women's magazines to City-page comment and corporate company image-building. Publicity in this sense is one specialised aspect of the wider role of public relations, which is defined by the Institute of Public Relations as "the deliberate, planned and sustained effort to establish and maintain mutual understanding between an organisation and its public." Publicity activities may, therefore, be carried out by company marketing personnel or public relations officers, by advertising agencies or by public relations consultants.

PROGRESS TEST 7

1. What are the five basic steps in campaign planning?   **(1–6)**
2. What methods are used in copy research?   **(10)**
3. How are readership classes normally defined?   **(14)**
4. What are the main problems in assessing "effective costs"? **(14–15)**
5. What are the most usual ways of determining advertising budgets?   **(19)**
6. What are the reasons for the development of private brands? **(24)**
7. What are the main reasons for special sales promotions?   **(30)**

PART THREE

ORGANISATION FOR MARKETING

CHAPTER VIII

ORGANISATION AND CONTROL

1. Organisation structure and control systems. There is no model organisation structure which will meet the requirements of all types of business. Organisation structures depend on many factors, *e.g.* the size of the business and its industrial classification, the markets it serves, its stage of growth, and the skills and experience of its people. There are, however, three distinctive features of the organisation of truly marketing-oriented companies:

(*a*) Certain specific marketing tasks, *e.g.* marketing research, advertising and promotion, sales and distribution, after-sales service, are co-ordinated under a single executive.

(*b*) Clear formal communications are established between the chief marketing executive and executives responsible for development, design and manufacturing and finance.

(*c*) Marketing performance is judged by profit and return on investment—not by volume of sales.

The number of marketing executives employed will vary. Small companies may not be able to justify the employment of specialists for every marketing task. A marketing orientation does not depend on the number of people employed in particular marketing specialisms but on conformity with the principles listed under (*a*), (*b*) and (*c*) above.

This chapter is concerned with the establishment of the information evaluation and control systems which guide a company towards the achievement of its marketing objectives and plans.

EVALUATION AND CONTROL

2. Evaluation and control mechanisms. A marketing system must have evaluation control and mechanisms built into it in order that actual performance may be measured against objectives and forecasted performance. Information indicating significant variances from plans must be fed back speedily to relevant decision points so that corrective action may be taken. Organisational structures with clear definitions of *authority, responsibility* and *lines of communication* are, therefore, an important element in any control system.

3. Reasons for variations from planned performance. Variations from planned performance will always arise because of the following factors:

(a) All plans are built on *imperfect information*.

(b) *Marketing decisions are complex* and there will usually be a large number of interacting objectives—failure to reach any single objective may have a bearing on the attainment of other objectives; *e.g.* in attempting to gain a given share of a market, profits may fall below target because additional sales expense has been incurred.

(c) *The marketing environment is constantly changing* and it is impossible to predict every eventuality.

(d) *Organisations are becoming bigger.* This leads to the involvement of more and more people who are linked by information systems rather than by personal contact; the range of products extends; the location of factories, offices, warehouses, becomes more diffuse.

(e) *Variations in performance in other systems,* such as production, personnel, or finance, affect marketing performance.

(f) *Performance depends not only on the company employees* but on the performance of wholesalers, retailers, advertising agencies and others, who can never be subject to the same degree of control.

4. The importance of targets. An effective control system depends on the setting on realistic goals or targets. Targets should be quantified whenever possible. It is almost impossible to evaluate performance against general statements of objectives. However, it is also more difficult to communicate intelligibly non-quantified objectives. Numerical targets make practicable the fixing of tolerances—the extent of permissible variance. It is only by establishing control limits that management by exception can be applied; otherwise every minor deviation at every point of time at which information is received will throw up problems of decision.

THE PROFIT CENTRE CONCEPT

5. Responsibility or profit centres. The increasing complexity of organisations and multiplicity of products is leading to devolution of responsibility. Closely controlled centralised operations are giving way to decentralised systems with greater emphasis on delegation. *Responsibility* centres are often set up, the responsibility for making a profit on particular operations being delegated to particular executives.

6. Types of profit centres. The whole marketing department may be treated as a profit centre. This would imply that goods are really being purchased from manufacturing departments and profits result from the difference between the cost of purchase plus sales expense and the revenue obtained from the market place. In this way, the chief marketing executive becomes responsible for achieving a given return on investment and will think in terms of *cost* and *revenue* rather than in terms of volume.

Profit centres may similarly be established for individual product lines or groups of products.

Sometimes, the profit centre concept is applied to types of customers or market segments, to branch offices or geographical sales areas or to channels of distribution.

7. Information and distribution costs. There is certainly a great need to pay more attention to the costs of distribution which, in many cases, are not only higher than the cost of manufacturing but represent more than half of the final selling price. Many existing accounting systems could be extended to provide more significant information on cost; sales representatives, for example, are frequently unaware of the cost of their calls, or the cost of providing special deliveries and services. Marketing management certainly needs to consider the various combinations of channels, products, promotional and sales effort, which will yield satisfactory return at the least cost. Information collection and distribution can itself be an unnecessary cost, however, and it is important to establish what information is needed, for whom, when, where and in what form. The speed of information output from computers makes it all the more necessary to determine information flow and needs precisely.

THE MAJOR BASES OF PERFORMANCE EVALUATION

8. Sales targets and budgets. These are both fundamental to overall performance evaluation.

(a) *Sales targets.* Based on market evaluation and resources available, overall targets should be set which lay down what is to be achieved in both the short and the long term.

(b) *Budgets.* A marketing budget agreed by top management should be drawn up to show the permissible cost in relation to achieved target. The budget is the major means of evaluating profit performance.

9. Long- and short-range budgets. A distinction should be made between *long-range budgets* covering 3, 5 or 10 years ahead in order to determine long-range capital, facility and manpower needs, based on an assessment of long-range plans for business growth, and *annual budgets* which are a control device for the year ahead.

Long-range budgets are very necessary if companies are to plan for growth and change. These budgets require an evaluation of the likely effect of external and internal events over the forward period, against the background of which new products will be launched. The budget will indicate the likely profitability of new and existing products, as well as market shares. Products which are likely to fall below given company profit objectives have to be analysed so that decisions may be taken on appropriate action—to modify, to increase sales effort, or to drop.

10. Quantifiable overall objectives. The company must establish clear long- and short-term objectives so that these may be incorporated in the overall budgets as well as in departmental budgets.

Important quantifiable objectives may be:

(a) gross and net sales figures;
(b) market shares;
(c) profit expressed in monetary terms and as a percentage of sales;
(d) turnover of capital inventory, and accounts receivable;
(e) return of investment on capital employed.

Profit on sales reflects performance in maintaining cost

control; turnover reflects the speed at which capital in the business is being worked. Return on investment—a most important yardstick—can be improved by reducing costs or using capital more effectively.

11. Other overall objectives. Other important objectives may not be so easily quantified, *e.g.*:

    (*a*) providing for manpower training and development;
    (*b*) providing for effective plant and manpower utilisation;
    (*c*) avoidance of excessive variations in level of business transacted;
    (*d*) maintenance of and/or improvement of market standing against competition;
    (*e*) providing for a satisfactory level of shareholder dividends in both short and long term;
    (*f*) providing for employee job satisfaction.

12. Responsibility budgeting. If profit, expense and revenue centres are established, and managers at various levels of an organisation are accountable for their performance in relation to budgets, it is important that the following conditions are observed:

    (*a*) The executive concerned should understand and agree the particular budget. Pursuing the notion of management by objectives, the executive would not only agree, he would participate in the decision and perhaps even construct his own objectives in line with major company objectives.

    (*b*) An executive who carries a responsibility for profits must have the authority to make necessary adjustments to programmes in order to reach the profit target.

    (*c*) Adequate information on performance should be available in the right form at the right time.

INFORMATION FOR MARKETING EVALUATION AND CONTROL

13. Reasons for information. The provision of relevant information at the right time to the right people is the basis of an evaluation and control system. Information is required to:

    (*a*) provide for evaluation and control of overall marketing performance;

(b) provide for evaluation and control of subfunctions and individuals within marketing departments or divisions;

(c) provide specific data for any necessary action in relation to products, marketing programmes or prices;

(d) provide information for salesmen.

14. Main types of marketing control analyses. The most commonly analysed information supplied for overall marketing analysis falls under six headings described in subsequent paragraphs:

(a) Sales analysis (**15**).
(b) Product share analysis (**17**).
(c) Distribution analysis (**18**).
(d) Sales force activity analysis (**19**).
(e) Cost and profit analysis (**20**).
(f) Advertising analysis (**23**).

15. Sales analysis: information. Sales managers tend to judge current performance by the volume of business and size of individual orders. Difficulties arise if the only information available regularly is aggregate orders. Information needs to be broken down much further for evaluation and control. Possible breakdown categories in terms of unit volume and sales revenue are:

(a) by products; these can be further separated if necessary into particular styles and sizes;
(b) by customer type or size;
(c) by sales territories;
(d) by channels of distribution;
(e) by terms of sale;
(f) by key outlets.

16. Sales analysis: standards. Information received must then be set against standards, *e.g.* annual forecasts, previous month's performance, last year's performance. It is also important to measure performance against opportunity and not just against the company's own past record. This requires supplementary information from the field and marketing research reports. Regular reports on marketing expenses by various categories will also be required if profit targets are to be met.

One of the problems frequently encountered in actual operations is that sales analysis data arrives too late for effective action. In volatile consumer markets, for example, detailed analysis six weeks after events may be much too late to enable effective corrective action to be taken.

17. Product share (brand position) analysis. Regular information on a company's own as well as competitive brand shares of the market is extremely valuable. Growth in volume business—or indeed in profits—is no guarantee of complete realisation of opportunities. A 3% improvement in volume is unsatisfactory set against an overall market growth of 15%. Apart from immediate lost profit opportunities, loss of market share may reflect on future business prospects. A change in brand leadership may mean considerable modification of plans. In certain fast-moving consumer markets, *e.g.* dairy and grocery, regular audits of brand share positions are undertaken by the A. C Nielsen Company and other specialist agencies (*see* III, 12). In industrial markets and consumer areas where the information is not readily available a company may have to devise its own arrangements for taking stock checks. High sales stocks in the warehouse of an agent or intermediary may indicate a high level of anticipated demand *or* a decline in demand at the next point along the chain. Stock-level information must, therefore, be supplemented by data on the estimated usage level and flow of products; a stock-piling of all brands, for example, may indicate a general recession, either cyclical or permanent.

18. Distribution analysis. It may be comparatively simple to codify outlets to reveal statistics on actual company transactions, but where products are transferred, say from wholesaler to retailer, it is more difficult to evaluate performance of particular links in the distribution chain. Information on stock levels, stock condition, order sizes, and selling effort at outlets where sales calls are not regularly made may be necessary. Again syndicated information is sometimes available from outside sources, but the sales force may be required to check on display activities or to ensure that inefficient systems of withdrawal from stock do not mean that the newest stock is used first. Old or damaged stock reflects more on the manufacturer than on the final supplier.

One of the great problems in distribution evaluation is to

establish standards of performance. As in other forms of
evaluation, reliable standards are needed for really effective
control. The problem of measuring the performance of
distribution points with which the company is not in direct
contact is obvious, but comparison of performance of wholesalers and agents on the basis of one year's figures against
another's is also inadequate. Does a 20% increase by one
wholesaler represent a greater effort than a 10% increase by
another? More attention should sometimes be paid to
establishing standards in relation to potential and constraints.
It may, for instance, be possible to measure performance of
various overseas agents by establishing relative potential
indices based on such information as total population, rural
and urban population, degree of industrialisation, educational
standards, and extent of communications and transport
systems in each region. Similar indices could, of course, be
developed for home markets.

19. Sales force activity analysis. Some of the previous
analyses give an indication of salesmen's performance, *e.g.*
sales by products in a particular territory. There are other
measurements which may be necessary. A salesman may
have tasks other than actually effecting a sale, such as display and service. Again, if action is to be taken to raise the
level of sales performance it may be useful to have information
on the following:

    (*a*) Number of calls per day.
    (*b*) Number of different calls per month.
    (*c*) Ratio of orders to calls.
    (*d*) Value of sales per call.
    (*e*) Time spent on non-selling activities.
    (*f*) Mileage covered in given periods—mileage per call.
    (*g*) New accounts opened.
    (*h*) Expenditure and cost of obtaining sales.

20. Cost and profit analysis: difficulties of allocation. Company costs might be said to cover basically manufacturing
costs and marketing costs. The allocation of manufacturing
costs raises problems but nothing like so great as those of
allocating marketing costs. Marketing, like manufacturing,
has the problem of overhead allocation, *e.g.* for managerial
salaries, but manufacturing costs are allocated to processes

and things manufactured, however arbitary the allocation may sometimes be in practice. The ultimate output of marketing is a sale, but it is difficult to determine the allocation to marketing processes. Products, salesmen, advertising, distributors—all contribute to sales but in ways which are difficult to quantify. Similarly additional cost in manufacturing is likely to yield a given output, but it is much more difficult to estimate the effect on sales revenue of hiring extra salesmen or increasing an advertising appropriation. Marketing costs can only be viewed in terms of absolute accuracy in total; individual activity costs provide a basis for revision of the balance of these costs.

21. Cost and profit analysis: methods. Nevertheless measurement depends on being able to examine both cost and revenue. Margins, for example, might be increased either by increasing sales more than expenses, or by reducing expense more than sales. It is difficult to adjust margins or to use budgets to regulate specific marketing activities unless, therefore, there is an attempt to break down marketing expenses. Cost and profit analysis are consequently carried out in three main ways:

(a) *By calculating gross margins for specific managerial units.* Gross margins are what remains after the cost of goods sold is deducted from sales revenue. Lower gross margins on certain products or in certain markets point to a need to investigate. Falling margins may, for example, indicate that there is something wrong with the marketing plan and marketing efforts may be badly directed.

(b) *By breaking down expenses into normal categories* such as salaries, rent, supplies, and comparing the expense against the gross profit of a profit centre.

(c) *By allocating all direct and indirect costs* to specific managerial units and setting these against profits. The units may be territories, customer groups or product groups. There are very considerable problems of allocation, *e.g.* when one salesman handles products from two or three different product groups or calls on two or three different customer groups. Similar problems arise in the case of corporate product advertising, billing, or mixed product-customer-type deliveries. Where product groups, outlet types, sales delivery arrangements and so on are reasonably well separated, it is possible and often very worth while to carry out this kind of analysis. The major

consideration is to ensure that the benefits of undertaking the
exercise exceed the costs.

22. Cost and profit analysis: interpretation. Interpretation
needs care since most cost allocations are arbitrary. Direct
costs are simple, *e.g.* cost of salesmen or advertising directly
associated with a product, but costs of space, management
salaries, taxes, corporate advertising present considerable
difficulties. Distribution cost analysis in its purest state can
rarely be the basis for an immediate decision. It is a yardstick—to some extent arbitrary—measuring relative performance and should be regarded as a guide to areas requiring
further investigation.

It may be found, for example, that by measuring total
sales achieved against quotas there seems to be one star
salesman in a team. A gross margin analysis by product
may reveal that the salesman's effort and expense have been
devoted mainly to an easy selling line which yields a lower
gross margin than other products. If sales targets and expense
budgets have been set on the basis of anticipated market
demand and an expectation of balanced sales across the range
of products, and if direct costs have been allocated on the
basis of actual expense incurred by having the salesman in
his territory, the unbalanced selling could result in both a
low gross profit and a small contribution to profit. This kind
of analysis would indicate, in this case, the need for more
balanced selling effort; in other cases there might be pointers
to the need for purely increased sales volume or reduction of
selling expense.

23. Advertising analysis and mark-up. Advertising evaluation has been covered previously (*see* VII, **13–15**) but attention
should be drawn to the fact that the costs of advertising are
frequently given unfavourable publicity while little mention
is made of the costs of effecting distribution and sales through
conventional channels by offering suitable margins of profit.
While there are very considerable variations and generalisations
in terms of all goods marketed are impossible, it would not be
unusual to find that the advertising of strongly promoted
foodstuffs may account for 5% of the final retail price against
20% for retail margins. Wholesale margins are far lower
and this explains why it sometimes is not only more effective

in terms of sales revenue but also cheaper in cost to arrange terms direct on a single margin with large retailers. Sums spent on research and development, too, are frequently insignificant compared with mark-up allowances.

Marketing costs are mainly fixed regardless of the level of the flow of goods—unlike the variable costs of manufacturing. Margins to intermediaries may be regarded as an economic cost, but they are not an accounting burden. If their role was taken over by company-owned wholesale warehouses and retail outlets, rents, salaries and running expenses generally would become a fixed cost or overhead.

24. Determining marketing expenses. Companies find it difficult to assess whether they should increase or decrease marketing expenses—or indeed at what level they should be fixed at all. It might be simple to consider the costs of each marketing activity—selling, advertising, marketing research, channel costs, order processing, product planning. The problem here is that each reacts on the other. A method of isolating functions has been described under advertising as the sales task approach (*see* VI, **4–5**). Other possible ways of investigating expense and effectiveness are as follows:

(*a*) Analysis of resources, results, marketing methods and expenditure of competitors.

(*b*) Analysis of customer attitudes and behaviour.

(*c*) Analysis of non-accounting statistical data, *e.g.* difference in results of advertising carried out under controlled experimental conditions.

(*d*) Analysis of the relative importance of marketing activities in relation to sales. Similarly analysis of expense within an activity should be measured, *e.g.* who is the least productive salesman (in terms of contribution to profit); which is the least productive form of advertising. This kind of approach would be used if profits were falling; it is a useful guide—but only a guide—when profits *and also* expenses are rising. Some attempts to reduce cost are unlikely to have any really significant effect, *e.g.* general requests to cut down on telephone calls or stationery.

25. Budgets and flexibility. From what has already been said (**8–12** above) it will be clear that, although sales budgets are essential and central to the company operation, variations in the constituents of the total marketing expenses have no inevitable consequence in terms of sales revenue. There is, therefore, room for flexibility in the light of unexpected happenings. It is important that a measure of flexibility in the constituents be maintained since there will always be some unexpected developments in market situations. Often these developments will require adjustments in the way marketing expense is used in order to reach the planned marketing objectives; sometimes unexpected opportunities to exceed planned objectives will arise. Production expense may be affected by changes in wage levels or materials cost, for example, but the budgetary changes necessary are less complex and more predictable than in marketing. Indeed, production budgets are most likely to be affected by changes in sales.

Flexibility in sales budgets should not lead to thinking in terms of immediate reduction of constituents such as advertising, as demand falls. A fall in demand would affect the production budget and it may indeed be necessary to *increase* sales effort beyond the point of marginal return on sales cost in order to absorb uneconomic production capacity. One budget must be seen in relation to another and none is more critical in its inter-related effect than the sales budget. An apparently high selling cost might be justified if the volume of sales generated were sufficient to enable high productivity machines to be installed in the factory leading to reduced manufacturing cost, thus greatly improving the contribution to overall profit.

26. Fixed costs and revenue. Most marketing costs are fixed, but variable costs are involved in activities such as short-term promotions, sales commissions, temporary salesmen. If a high fixed cost in selling is combined with a high fixed cost in manufacturing, the dangers of a fall in profit (resulting from increased wages, rents, reduced demand, falling prices) are clear; diversification, rigorous product development policies, and a drive to differentiate products might be expected in circumstances of this kind.

27. Market development and investment. Although emphasis has been laid on the importance of comparing performances of products, of sales personnel, and of channels on the basis of profit contribution, it should be stressed that low contributions may arise because of the need to invest in sales training, or in cultivating certain intermediaries, *e.g.* voluntary group wholesalers, just as much as from the need to invest in product development and market introduction.

28. Financial reports and relevance. The rapid speed of punched card and computerised systems means that sophisticated information can be made available quickly. Consider the range of data which could be obtained from drawing up a product and a customer code for computer processing on the following lines:

(a) *Product.*

  (i) Product line, *e.g.* filter paper.
  (ii) Product size, *e.g.* 3 cm.
  (iii) Product type, *e.g.* circles.
  (iv) Product grade, *e.g.* 4.
  (v) Product price, *e.g.* £0·055.
  (vi) Product quantity, *e.g.* 12 × 100.

(b) *Customer.*

  (i) Name and address, *e.g.* Bryce and Co. Ltd., 29 Warren St., Tonbridge.
  (ii) Industrial or business classification, *e.g.* chemical and allied industries.
  (iii) Size by potential sales revenue, *e.g.* £10,000 p.a.
  (iv) Sales department, *e.g.* 4.
  (v) Salesman, *e.g.* 6.

The possible combinations of information would be too much for an individual to digest and it is, therefore, important to provide the right data for the right level at the right time.

The product manager concerned with product profit contribution may require summary reports by size, design, quality, revenue and margin. From this he might see slow-moving lines, uneven spread of sales, unexpected margins. More detailed reports may be necessary to follow through on significant variations from anticipated results.

The field sales manager is concerned not so much with profit contribution on single products as with volume or revenue targets and controllable expense. He may, therefore, need information on sales progress by territory and a considerable range of individual expense items such as office and equipment depreciation, salesmen's cars, stationery supplies. hotel bills, clerical salaries. The salesman, on the other hand, would be unable to control variable expenses apart from his own travelling, hotel and entertainment bills. His area manager may need a regular record of these expenses, but the salesman himself is primarily concerned with a record of sales and deliveries on his territory—in total by product and by individual account—plus, perhaps, records of outstanding customer debts.

29. Reports from field sales forces. Two problems arising from the various information systems described are, firstly, that there is a *time lag* between the event and the reporting of the event; and secondly, that the information is in *quantitative* terms. Supplementary verbal information may be necessary.

To remedy these defects salesmen are usually asked to make periodic reports on their field activities to area managers who similarly may provide reports for more senior executives. The frequency and detail of such reports must be carefully considered in the light of their value as evaluation and decision-making aids. Not infrequently very detailed daily sales reports from representatives contain information which is not really required or is available from other sources—and the compilation of these reports reduces the time available for selling and/or planning selling calls.

Well-planned field reports may, however, provide faster or more extensive information on such matters as the following:

(a) Number of calls made on particular days.
(b) Sales made or not made, with some explanation.
(c) Economy of routeing.
(d) Localised competitive activities.
(e) Significant customer or potential customer developments.
(f) Details of complaints on, for example, product performance, delivery.

30. Possible effects of sales reports. Field sales reports may lead to more effective operation in the following ways:

(a) By indicating the need for urgent training, motivation, or other remedial action.
(b) By acting as a constant reminder to the salesman or field sales executive that each day or week or month targets must be met if the annual target is to be reached.

(c) By providing fast information on the progress of special presentations or campaigns or on sales tactics which are proving particularly successful.

(d) By giving information on such matters as the progress of product tests, special display activities, technical servicing.

31. Communication, evaluation and control. It will be seen that much of the information required for evaluation and control is passing along formal organisational channels. An inherent danger here is that information can be misunderstood or distorted giving rise to suspicions, conflict and low morale. Marketing is an activity involving a particularly large number of informal groupings and personnel with wide individual differences. A purely bureaucratic, mechanistic approach to objectives, control and evaluation is, therefore, likely to lead to low morale and failure to meet imposed objectives. In a bureaucratic control system sales reports, for example, can become mainly alibis—means of protecting the individual or the group. The purpose of control and evaluation must, therefore, be understood and accepted by the participants in the system so that they constructively participate in achieving and setting objectives which satisfy not only the company and its executives' hierarchy, but the needs and aspirations of informal groups and individuals.

PROGRESS TEST 8

1. What are the main reasons for variations from plans in marketing? **(3)**

2. What are profit centres? **(5, 6)**

3. How might a company express its overall objectives? **(10)**

4. What are the main types of marketing control analyses? **(14)**

5. Why are there special problems in the allocation of costs to marketing activities? **(20)**

6. What are the three ways in which cost and profit analyses are carried out? **(21)**

7. In what way might information for product managers differ from information for field sales managers? **(28)**

8. What is the purpose of field sales reports? **(29)**

E

CHAPTER IX

CHANNELS OF DISTRIBUTION

DEFINITION AND TYPES

1. Channels defined. The term "channels of distribution" refers to the system of marketing institutions through which goods or services are transferred from the original producers to the ultimate users or consumers. Most frequently a physical product transfer is involved, but sometimes an intermediate marketing institution may take title to goods without actually handling them.

2. Marketing institutions: types and functions. There is a very wide range of marketing institutions which carry out a variety of functions along the distribution channels. Amongst the most important are the following:

(a) *Retailers.* Independent traders operating outlets selling "at retail" to household consumers.

(b) *Wholesalers.* Independent traders who sell "at whole-sale" to other business organisations either for the purpose of resale or for business use. The terms "distributor" and "jobber" are frequently used in American literature to describe an exactly similar type of trader. (Occasionally the terms have a different meaning, *e.g.* American jobbers dealing in automobile components and packed-meat products frequently buy from distributors who own warehouses and then sell to retail outlets.)

(c) *Agents and brokers.* Organisations who operate at the wholesale level, but who buy or sell *on behalf of others.* They normally earn their profit from commission payments made in return for their part in negotiating business transactions.

(d) *Facilitating institutions.* Organisations which neither take title to goods nor negotiate purchases or sales but assist the marketing activities of manufacturers and the institutions mentioned in (a) to (c) above. Examples include:

    (i) commodity trading exchanges;
    (ii) trade associations;
    (iii) advertising and marketing research agencies;
    (iv) credit service organisations and finance companies;
    (v) freight carriers.

118

BASIC CHANNEL DECISIONS

3. Direct selling. Some producers sell direct to end users. This type of operation is found more frequently in the marketing of industrial goods and services than in marketing to domestic consumers. Door-to-door selling and mail order, however, are examples of direct consumer marketing.

4. Reasons for the use of direct selling. Factors which stimulate direct marketing are as follows:

(a) The need to demonstrate a technical product, to supervise tests, to undertake complicated and perhaps lengthy negotiations, or to provide specialised after-sales service.

(b) The lack of active selling by intermediaries.

(c) Inability to persuade existing channels to carry or merchandise stock.

(d) Unduly *high intermediary profit margins* which might give rise to cost and price advantages under a direct marketing system.

(e) Inability of intermediaries to effect physical transportation.

(f) Industrial market structures with comparatively few potential buyers—often geographically concentrated.

5. Reasons against the use of direct selling. Factors which inhibit direct marketing are as follows:

(a) *Lack of financial resources.*

(b) *The need to use capital* to provide a better *return on investment*; *e.g.* a manufacturer of a range of games would under most circumstances utilise available capital more efficiently in ways other than by engaging large numbers of salesmen to call on thousands of potential occasional domestic purchasers buying in small quantities.

(c) *Lack of "know-how"* in effecting final distribution. Retail store management calls for special skills, *e.g.* in buying for resale, in shelf-space allocation, in organising a predominantly female and often part-time labour force.

(d) *Lack of a sufficiently wide assortment* of own products to operate economically. Sales of individual items at retail are affected markedly by the assortment available.

(e) The existence of channels which are designed specifically to deal in *assortments and to break bulk.*

(f) A consumer market structure with *large numbers of potential buyers geographically scattered.*

6. Basic marketing processes. Marketing involves various basic processes:

(a) Bringing buyers and sellers into *contact*.

(b) Offering a *choice of goods* sufficient to gain the interest and meet the needs of buyers.

(c) Persuading potential buyers to develop *favourable attitudes* to a particular products.

(d) Maintaining an *acceptable price level*.

(e) *Physically distributing goods* from manufacturing points to buying or use locations with the possible provision of additional storage points.

(f) Effecting an *adequate flow of sales*.

7. Channel decisions: effectiveness and cost. Channel decisions must, therefore, ultimately be based on the realisation that failure to delegate these functions listed in para **6** above to intermediaries will increase costs, and that increased costs must be justified by appropriate economic advantages in terms of profit, market penetration or other company objectives.

8. Multi-channel decisions. A producer may decide to use more than one channel system in order to reach his market. A large-scale manufacturer of soaps and detergents may, for example, decide to market products to both domestic consumers and industrial users. To reach domestic markets most effectively and economically the following decisions may be taken:

(a) Terms of sale for large chain groups will be negotiated by senior management direct. Delivery will be made to individual stores. Salesmen will have access to individual stores to arrange displays and to take orders under conditions negotiated centrally.

(b) Other large retail outlets will be sold to direct by salesmen allocated to particular territories.

(c) Salesmen will sell to wholesalers whose main resale activity will be concentrated on smaller retail outlets.

To reach a wide range of industrial users it may be decided to effect distribution by various channels. Certain sectors of the market, *e.g.* restaurants, canteens, will be reached through well-established wholesalers. Other sectors, *e.g.* textile manufacturers, will be sold to on a direct basis, perhaps because of a need to demonstrate technical superiority of specialised products or because a major share of the total market can be obtained by calling on a relatively small number of outlets in a limited number of geographical concentrations.

RETAILING

9. The functions of retailing. Retailing is the final link in the chain of distribution of consumer products. The function retailers perform are the consequence of the separation of distance, time and information between producers and consumers (*see* I, **8**). Hence all retailers are involved in assisting in the physical movement of goods and in effecting a change of ownership. Retailers also hold stocks so that goods are available when required by the consumer, thus contributing to the reduction of the time separation. Retailers pass on information on products to consumers and back to producers, so reducing the information separation.

10. Methods of retailing. The manner in which retailing functions are performed differs widely; *e.g.* some retailers have van delivery services, some rely on counter selling, others on self-service; some retailers hold wide stock assortments, others hold very limited ranges; some retailers advertise in the press and run their own sales promotions, while others rely on personal service.

Retailing functions are performed by non-store (*see* **11–13**) and store establishments (*see* **14–36**).

NON-STORE ESTABLISHMENTS

11. Types of non-store establishments. Examples of non-store establishments are mail order houses, vending machines, door-to-door sales organisations, mobile shops, market traders and credit traders, but these outlets only account for a very small proportion of retail business. The most significant developments in non-store retailing are considered in **12** and **13** below.

12. Mail order. Over 3% of total trade is now conducted by mail order and the six largest mail order organisations account for two-thirds of mail order business transacted. Household textiles, soft furnishings and footwear represent their greatest volume of business. The following may be included among the reasons for growth:

(a) *Increased trading in branded goods* known and accepted by potential customers.

(b) *Congestion in major shopping centres*, with parking and transport problems for shoppers.

(c) *More married women in employment*, with less time to spend on shopping or unable to visit shops during their shorter opening hours.

(d) *Improved organisation* by mail order companies—central buying, better stock control, more effective use of advertising. This has led to higher operating margins.

13. Door-to-door selling. The most interesting developments in this type of operation are associated with specific companies, *e.g.* the "Tupperware" party-selling system and Avon Cosmetics, which use home selling by part-time women representatives paid on a commission basis. In both cases major contributory factors to success have been the development of a leisurely social climate during the selling process and the provision of ample opportunity for the demonstrating and testing of products.

RETAIL STORES

Store establishments account for the major proportion of retail business; their organisation and operation is considered in some detail in **14–36** below.

14. Methods of classification of retail stores. Retail stores may be classified as follows:

(a) *By type or range of goods offered.* Some stores offer only goods in a highly specialised category, *e.g.* furniture, millinery, meat; others offer a wide range of different types of goods, *e.g.* a combination of food, drapery, hardware.

(b) *By the functions performed.* Some stores offer goods

only by self-service; some offer delivery as well as self-service; others offer counter service and delivery.

(c) *By size.* Measurement of this may be based on the number of employees or the sales turnover.

(d) *By ownership, e.g.* independent, co-operative.

(e) *By location, e.g.* rural, urban.

These classifications are all important in specific marketing situations, but the present purpose is to examine general trends in retailing. The majority of shops in Britian are small in size and unincorporated, *i.e.* owned by one individual or a partnership. The share of total retail trade transacted in shops which are part of an incorporated business, *i.e.* owned by private or public companies, is, however, constantly growing. The position of the independent (unincorporated) tradesman is first examined (**15**) and there follows a more detailed treatment of the developments in incorporated retail establishments (**16–36**).

15. The independent trader. The majority of shops in Britain are small and independently owned, but the percentage of total trade these small establishments transact is constantly diminishing. Loss of market share is most outstanding in the case of grocery products.

(a) *Difficulties* encountered by the small trader include the following:

(i) Price competition from multiple organisations, who enjoy bulk buying advantages as well as other organisational economies of scale. There is no longer the protection of resale price maintenance.

(ii) Lack of specialist expertise in the various functions of retailing, *e.g.* buying, display, accounting, stock control.

(iii) Lack of capital to invest in modernisation, *e.g.* provision of self-service facilities, accounting machines.

(iv) Location. Small traders usually lack the advantage of being in a major shopping centre where the customer is free to exercise choice over a wide range of purchases (but *see* (b)(ii)).

(v) Increased car ownership and the involvement of husbands in both buying and transportation tends to draw shoppers to the larger stores in the major shopping centres.

(b) *Advantages* the small trader can offer customers include the following:

(*i*) Personal relationship with customers.

(*ii*) Convenience in being located near customers' houses or place of work.

(*iii*) Stock not necessarily limited to fast-moving items but catering for more individual needs.

(*iv*) Greater flexibility in arranging shopping hours.

(*v*) Overheads can be kept small because of siting, low labour cost, etc.

(*vi*) Greater flexibility in offering credit.

(*vii*) More flexibility in providing delivery service.

INCORPORATED RETAIL BUSINESSES

Incorporated businesses are retailing establishments owned by public and private companies; their organisation and the main trends in their development are examined in **16–36** below.

16. Multiple organisations: chain stores. Chain stores are groups of retail stores of a similar type with a common ownership and some degree of centralised control. Multiples were defined in the 1950 and 1957 Censuses as retail organisations, other than a co-operative society, with ten or more branches. In the 1961 Census retail organisations with five to nine branches were described as "small multiples." Multiples normally concentrate on a limited range of merchandise, *e.g.* groceries, furnishings, clothing, shoes. Variety chains are exceptions, *e.g.* Woolworths, British Home Stores; retail chains handling a diversity of goods.

NOTE: Census statistics are not always directly comparable. For example, stores change in ownership category or in the range or type of business they transact between censuses.

17. Growth in multiples' share in trade. The share of total retail business transacted by multiple organisations has been growing very rapidly since 1950; very considerable gains have been recorded in almost every trade with just a few notable exceptions, *e.g.* butchers, newsagents, confectioners and tobacconists, greengrocers. The following table extracted from the 1961 Census Report illustrates the growth pattern of the multiples' share of trade:

	1950	1961	1961 *share* as % of 1950 *share*
Boot and shoe shops	55·7	64·4	116
Grocery and provisions	19·9	26·7	134
Radio and/or electrical goods shops	13·1	35·8	273
Bread and flour confectioners	15·6	30·9	198
Chemists	32·7	36·1	110
Dairymen	26·9	36·0	134
Off-licences	31·1	51·8	166

It is difficult to give more up-to-date figures as the last Census was taken in 1961. However, recent trends can be seen from the following figures extracted from the Index of Retail Sales, where the multiples' growing share in retail trade is shown by means of index numbers (1961 is taken as the base year at 100).

	1964	1968
All businesses	113	133
Food	112	133
Clothing and footwear	110	127
Miscellaneous non-food	114	138
Durable goods shops	116	135
Departmental stores	113	132
Mail order business	142	204

Multiples have flourished particularly in central shopping areas and their location, as well as price advantages and stock arrangements, has probably contributed greatly to their success. At the same time, it is clear that customer resistance to more impersonal selling has been breaking down—a fact well demonstrated by the spectacular growth of supermarkets and self-service. Supermarkets are defined as self-service shops with a full range of food products, a minimum sales floor area of 2000 square feet and at least three checkouts.

18. The battle for shelf space. As multiples grow into regional and national organisations they present new problems to the manufacturers whose products are handled by them. Their large share of business transactions means that major manufacturers may be able to restrict very considerably the number of actual selling calls made, but the need to acquire

shelf space and display becomes more vital. So much is
ultimate movements of goods (and profit) associated with
shelf space that major retailing organisations—especially
supermarket operators—are more and more turning to assessing
stock assortments in such terms as sales per square (or linear)
foot of space, or gross margin per unit of space per unit of
time. Advertising and sales promotion schemes—particularly
the latter—are becoming more necessary to gain appropriate
space allocation and accelerate movement of goods out of
retail stores (*see* II, **11**; III, **27**; and VI).

In the final resort, however, the multiple organisation is
concerned with long-run profit, and margins are as important
as stock turnover. The more dominant multiples become in
trade share, the more likely it is that they will be able to
exert pressure on manufacturers' margins.

19. Private branding. Pressure on margins may be increased by the introduction of retailers' own private brands.
Privately branded products are almost always sold on the
basis of price. These private brands are rarely manufactured
by the retailer organisation but are supplied by both small
and large manufacturers frequently in addition to their own
branded products. Manufacturers may decide to supply
privately branded goods on the argument that spare capacity
can be utilised or larger runs operated, margins being kept
low by selling at prices sufficient to cover or slightly exceed
marginal costs. Unless the retailer has a quality control
organisation there may be the temptation to lower quality
standards; many private brands are certainly variable in
quality. The argument of lower costs incurred by the manufacturer does not apply to all types of products, however,
and is generally only valid in the case of products where there
is a very large margin allowed normally for advertising
and promotion. A manufacturer may also be prepared to
supply private brands on the argument that, if he doesn't,
a competitor will. The potential dangers to his own brands
are, of course, obvious.

20. Marks and Spencer: the St Michael brand. In some
cases, private brands were developed to overcome the problems
of uniform pricing imposed by resale price maintenance, but

the practice has grown since the abolition of R.P.M. The outstanding example of private brand marketing with rigid specifications and quality control is the Marks and Spencer operation (22). The "St Michael" label has been used to create a distinctive quality/value for money image. No competing brands are sold and marketing policy is not based on providing the cheapest product but on satisfying the needs of a large but well-defined market segment.

21. Principles of chain store operations. Significant general principles of chain store operations include the following:

(a) *Large volume movement and a high break-even point.* Success, therefore, depends largely on siting.

(b) *Uniformity*—store fascias, lay-out and operational policies.

(c) *Concentration on fast-moving lines*—popular manufacturer's brands or private brands.

(d) *Centralised buying.*

(e) *Minimum customer service* (*cf*. departmental stores, 22).

(f) *Group advertising* and promotional activities.

(g) *Low prices.*

DEPARTMENTAL STORES

22. Characteristics of departmental stores. The departmental store is really a collection of "shops," under one roof and ownership, each shop or department specialising in selling a special range of goods, *e.g.* clothing, furniture, footwear, cosmetics, electrical goods. Each department normally buys separately, exercises its own stock control and sets its own merchandising policy. There are, therefore, few economies of scale in terms of supply. The advantages must lie in providing service and convenience to customers under a general "house image."

23. Customer service. Customer service advantages may include the following:

(a) Provision of wide range of specialised goods in one location.

(b) Freedom to move around store to view.

(c) Provision of special services such as restaurants, telephones.

(*d*) Simplified credit systems—a range of purchases posted to a single account with various methods of deferred payment. Credit facilities are particularly useful in the case of higher-priced items such as furniture, or for irregularly purchased goods such as clothing and kitchenware which are outside the housewife's weekly shopping budget.

24. General principles of departmental store operations. Significant general principles of departmental store operations also include the following:

(*a*) *Siting* in major shopping centres in urban locations.

(*b*) Fairly extensive *local advertising* and specialised promotions frequently in the form of special "sales."

(*c*) *Delivery services.*

(*d*) *Staff trained* in handling specialised merchandise.

(*e*) *Provision of house services, e.g.* carpet laying, curtain fitting.

(*f*) *Occasional leasing of space* for "shops within shops"; space leased to manufacturers, *e.g.* Berkertex and Jaeger.

(*g*) *Trading-up in price* to compensate for services provided and high overhead structure.

25. Share of retail trade. In order to overcome the problem of lack of economy of scale in purchasing there has been a movement to create departmental chains. Sales of departmental organisations with ten or more stores represented 21% of total departmental store sales in 1961 as against 14% in 1950. The share of total retail business transacted by departmental stores has, however, remained at a fairly constant 5% for more than 20 years. Failure to make progress can be attributed partly to:

(*a*) growth of more specialised multiples;

(*b*) lack of flexibility in operation—not least in management structure;

(*c*) limitations of range of goods carried within particular departments.

26. Characteristics of variety stores. A variety store is one which handles a wide assortment of goods not necessarily related to each other, *e.g.* toys, cosmetics, sugar confectionery, hardware. It may be independently owned but is usually owned by a private or public company. A group of variety stores may, therefore, constitute a chain or multiple. Characteristics of variety stores include the following:

(a) *Handling of a wide range of unrelated goods* with customer opportunity to walk round store freely.
(b) *Preponderance of "convenience" or "impulse" goods* of low unit price.
(c) *Absence of credit and delivery service.*
(d) *Siting* in major shopping centres.
(e) *Counter service* and counter display.
(f) *Very limited direct advertising.*

27. Recent trends. Originally variety stores such as Woolworth operated mainly on the principle of low prices—the "bargain" store. More recently, there has been some evidence of extension of the lines stocked to include higher-priced items such as cameras, radios, clothing, kitchen furniture. In some cases there are indications of trading-up. Stocking of more expensive items and trading-up can be seen in the Woolworth operation but more particularly in such chain variety outlets as Littlewoods and British Home Stores. The Marks and Spencer variety chain, as has been previously indicated (**15**), is unique in its adherence to a single brand with rigid control of specification and quality.

28. Buying practices. The variety chain invariably has a centralised purchasing organisation but there are wide differences in the delegation of purchasing power to individual stores. The Woolworth central buying organisation, for example, may negotiate contract prices and keep store managers informed, but the individual store and district managers are free to make their own purchasing decisions and to negotiate with manufacturers. Marks and Spencer store managers do not have this negotiation freedom and are concerned only with the regulation of quantity and assortment of specified goods from specified sources.

CO-OPERATIVE SOCIETIES

29. Early developments. The Co-operative movement began in Rochdale in 1844 and was based on the notion that consumers should themselves control production and distribution in order to eliminate the waste of a competitive capitalist system. Dividends were to be paid out from trading surpluses in proportion to purchases made. Each retail society was to have its own area of trading free from competition from another retail society.

30. Later difficulties. The movement progressed fairly well up to the 1930s, but has more recently encountered great difficulties. As the members control the societies there have been tremendous differences in the attitude to change. Consequently many retail societies have stagnated while others have made notable progress. Attention is drawn to the *Co-operative Independent Commission Report* of 1958. It should be noted that Co-operative Societies were pioneers in the two most significant changes which have occurred in the pattern of retail trading, *viz.* the introduction of self-service and the rise of supermarkets.

Failure to keep pace with competition, however, may be attributed to the following factors:

(*a*) *Poor management.* This stems first from the inefficiency of many management committees consisting of members with no business expertise—committees which are difficult to change because there is usually insufficient organised voting power to replace ineffective members. There is also often a lack of managerial skill in executive store managers because of poor selection, lack of training facilities and inadequate financial incentives.

(*b*) *Poor service,* which stems from poor management.

(*c*) *Lack of integrated policy* between production and distribution. Individual societies have not always supported the Co-operative factories distributing the products through the Co-operative Wholesale Societies in England and Scotland. In turn, there has been a lack of marketing policy and direction in manufacturing and wholesaling organisations. Steps are now being taken to recruit more highly paid experienced marketing experts, and as the C.W.S. has increasingly become involved in the financing of many retail societies a greater measure of control of goods handled at retail is becoming possible.

(*d*) *Lack of member loyalty.* The original notion that members would shop exclusively from Co-operative Stores was inpracticable. The increasing attractions of competitive retail outlets have shattered any remaining illusions of large-scale

exclusive store loyalty. The attraction of a dividend paid
annually has decreased as more immediate benefits have been
offered by other retailers.

(e) *The high degree of decentralisation* has made the economies
of scale and improved efficiency techniques of more closely-knit
large retail organisations difficult to effect.

(f) *Problems in relation to pricing policy and dividends*, provision of capital reserves and accounting procedures generally.

31. Share of retail trade. Co-operative Societies accounted
for 11% of retail trading according to the 1961 Census as
against 12·3% in 1957. There are strong indications that
the percentage is still falling. One of the main reasons is the
slow rate of conversion to self-service. The main strength
of Co-operatives is in food products, where they run fairly
level with other multiples, each enjoying some 25% of the
total. It is significant that Co-operatives are especially
strong in the distribution of milk and coal, where store merchandising is of little importance, whereas the new multiples
have greater success in footwear and clothing, mainly because
of their more effective merchandising and closer integration
of manufacturing/marketing policy. It is also significant
that Co-operative shares of footwear and clothing business are
lowest in the biggest population centres where multiples are
also much more strongly represented in terms of sites.

MANUFACTURER-OWNED OUTLETS

32. Arguments against vertical integration. Vertical integration—complete control from production through to ultimate
distribution—is comparatively rare for the following reasons:

(a) Most companies prefer to utilise limited assets—of skill
as well as finance—in specialised activities from which they
have the greatest of opportunity of profits.

(b) Rarely is it possible to provide a satisfactory assortment
of goods in retail outlets from a single manufacturer's range.

(c) Selling to other (now competitive) retail outlets becomes
difficult and the rate of retail growth must therefore correspond
closely to the rate of manufacturing growth.

(d) The number and range of retail distribution points is
inevitably curtailed.

33. Arguments for vertical integration. Arguments in favour of an integrated manufacturing/retailing organisation include the following:

(a) Possible cost savings. The elimination of middlemen margins may provide the opportunity for pricing advantages.

(b) Provision of more effective service. This argument might apply particularly in the case of certain technical products or "do it yourself" items, e.g. Singer sewing machines, Marley tiles.

(c) More effective merchandising and broad line stocking. The problems of introducing new or slow-moving items to large retail outlets have been previously mentioned (see IX, 18 above)

(d) The growth of large-scale integrated organisations dominating distribution of a product range, e.g. footwear, petrol, alcoholic drinks, men's clothing, pharmaceuticals. If a manufacturer has difficulty in gaining adequate retail distribution because many retail outlets are owned by his competitors, he may have to protect his interests by investing in retailing; e.g. Ranks flour is used in shops owned by British Bakeries, Spillers flour in United Bakeries shops.

DISCOUNT STORES

34. Characteristics of discount stores. Discount stores are still comparatively small in number in the UK, but have become a major factor in retailing in the USA. Basic features of discount store operations are as follows:

(a) *Low price* is the major appeal.

(b) *There is a low mark-up* with minimum customer service (mainly self-service). Gross margins on durable items and clothing may, for example, be up to 10% below those operated in departmental, variety or multiple stores.

(c) Purchases are mostly for *cash*.

(d) *Stores are usually very large* (in the USA normally over 50,000 sq. ft. and sometimes exceeding over 100,000 sq. ft.).

(e) *"Hard" goods* are the major lines stocked, but some discount houses have added foods and other "soft" goods.

35. Recent trends. It is interesting to note that there is already evidence in the USA that many discount houses are departing from the original warehouse-like, self-service, cash-down operation, and moving towards the provision of credit financing arrangements, sales attendance and more attractive furnishings.   The ultimate outcome of the operation will probably be that competitive retail outlets will reduce margins and discount stores will increase them.

36. Difficulties in classifying retail stores.   It will now be evident that classification in terms of size, service and range of products carried may be possible in general terms but there is a great deal of overlap. There are small and large co-operatives, there are independent traders who provide counter service while others have self-service, and there has been a reduction in the number of stores carrying a limited range of highly specialised items.   The dairy sells sausages, the off-licence sells confectionery, the multiple food store, perhaps, sells paint and kitchenware.

WHOLESALING

37. The economic purposes.   Wholesalers may be said to provide the economic utilities of time, place and possession which may lead to economies in distribution—adequate stocks to be available at the right time in a convenient location.

38. Merchant wholesalers.   Most wholesalers fall into this category—they buy and sell goods, taking title to the goods, then deriving profit from the marginal difference between the price at which they buy and the price at which they sell. Most merchant wholesaler undertake the following additional functions:

   (*a*) They store goods.
   (*b*) They undertake some advertising or promotional activity.
   (*c*) They fix selling prices.
   (*d*) They arrange credit terms.
   (*e*) They make delivery.
   (*f*) They offer advisory services.

39. Trade margins.   Buying and selling margins vary widely, fluctuating in general with the risk carried and the range and effectiveness of functions performed.   If a wholesaler, for example, stocks expensive durable goods which require technical service, his margins must be sufficiently high to compensate for these activities. It would, therefore, be reasonable to expect that the manufacturer of refrigerators who expected a wholesaler to carry high stocks and provide servicing facilities would give much higher margins than a manufacturer of fast-moving canned food products. Sometimes, however, margins remain at a traditional level when original functions such as stocking and servicing are no longer carried out.   This state of affairs may occur either because manufacturers are slow to recognise changed circumstances or because they are reluctant to take action in case they lose ground to competitors offering more favourable terms.

40. Size and specialisation. Some merchant wholesalers handle a wide range of general merchandise, but the majority specialise to a greater or lesser extent. Many are small and operate within a comparatively small geographical radius, but a number (particularly in certain trades such as grocery) are large and have regional and even national distribution. Examples of the various types of specialised wholesalers with a limited range of functions are described in **41–46** below.

41. Cash and carry wholesalers. These are at present mainly concerned with grocery products. They offer neither credit nor delivery services and, as a result, operate on lower margins.

42. Rack jobbers. This is a recent development of truck wholesaling, previously limited mainly to perishable goods which may be collected from producers and delivered direct to retailers without the need for storage facilities. Rack jobbers are beginning to carry out a truck wholesaling function in supermarkets, where they may take over responsibility for maintaining stocks and display of particular lines on particular shelves.

43. Brokers. Brokers negotiate sales between sellers and buyers. They take neither title to nor possession of goods. Profits are derived either on the basis of an average commission on value, on a commission on volume, or on a pre-determined fee based on sales. Brokers usually specialise in narrow ranges of products, *e.g.* sugar, tea, cotton piece goods. Specialisation is to be expected since their value lies in the deep knowledge of particular markets and market conditions.

44. Factors or commission merchants. Factors do not buy goods, nor do they take title, but they do take possession and provide warehousing and handling facilities. Payment is normally by fixed commission. Whereas the broker represents buyer and/or seller, factors represent the seller only. Factors are most commonly found where there are many small producers and a few large central markets through which products are resold, *e.g.* agricultural products.

45. Selling agents. Selling agents are most commonly found where small manufacturers wish to be relieved of marketing responsibility so that very limited financial assets may be devoted exclusively to production. The selling agent usually works closely, therefore, with the manufacturer over long periods, having complete responsibility for all sales. He accordingly sometimes supplies advice on style and design. Some sales agents work for one principal but the majority carry a range of manufacturers' products, normally of a complementary kind. Selling agents sometimes carry the risks of credit loss and have considerable discretion over selling prices.

46. Manufacturers' agents. A manufacturers' agent differs from a selling agent in the following ways:

(*a*) He handles products in a limited geographical area only.

(*b*) He usually handles several manufacturers' lines, although these are normally by terms of the agreement non-competitive.

(*c*) He has little if any freedom to negotiate terms of sale and price.

(*d*) He has usually little control of product styling design.

(*e*) He is rarely involved in credit collection and risk.

Manufacturers' agents commonly have warehousing facilities from which local deliveries are made, goods being held on consignment. Commissions are normally much smaller than in the case of selling agents since the functions performed and risks involved are smaller. Agency organisations vary in size, although most are comparatively small. They flourish particularly in circumstances where small manufacturers are

endeavouring to tackle complex or widespread markets, *e.g.*
industrial supplies and overseas markets. Automobile distribution is, however, conducted mainly through large-scale
agencies who have exclusive area selling rights and usually,
in return, act for one manufacturer only.

47. Wholesaler-sponsored voluntary groups or chains. The
growth of large-scale retail operators is a threat to small
independent traders and to wholesalers alike. To counter
the threat a number of wholesalers have combined to provide
a central staff, while retaining control of the individual
business. The central staff provides various services to all
retailers who subscribe to the group. Members are expected
to purchase a high percentage of their goods from a group
wholesaler. Services provided by the central staff may include
the following:

(*a*) *Advertising and promotional support* under a group name,
e.g. "Mace," "Spar," "Centra," "V.G." Special promotions
are arranged with manufacturers.

(*b*) *Advice on merchandising*, display, lay-out, equipment.

(*c*) *Advice on retailing efficiency techniques*, stock ranges,
accounting, capital utilisation.

(*d*) *Access* to private label products.

(*e*) *Financial assistance* for shop improvements.

(*f*) *Preferential insurance* coverage terms.

(*g*) *Special buying terms* resulting from negotiation of bulk
buying contracts.

It should be noted that the voluntary group wholesaler
movement lays great emphasis on assisting members to sell
more effectively and enhance profits by greater all-round
efficiency, and is not merely or primarily offering goods at
cheaper prices. This movement has so far been most promi-
nent in the grocery field, but may well spread to other retail
outlets.

48. Retail-sponsored buying groups. Attempts have been
made in various retail trades to establish group buying arrangements on a voluntary basis in order to obtain advantages of
larger-scale purchases. Groups are usually formed on a
very local basis, sometimes with a central warehouse and
office being acquired. The progress of the movement in the
UK has been much slower than in some European countries

and it seems unlikely that this form of group buying will become a major factor in the foreseeable future.

CHANNEL-CHOICE PROBLEMS FOR THE MANUFACTURER

Channel choice must be considered in the light of market coverage and control, product characteristics and market characteristics.

49. Market coverage and control. Distribution policy can be based on the following systems:

(a) *Intensive distribution.* This is a term used in different ways: *viz.* limited geographical distribution as opposed to national distribution; maximum distribution to all outlets of a specific type, *e.g.* chemists, grocers; maximum distribution to every possible type of outlet.

(b) *Selective distribution.* This involves selection by the producer of the types of retail outlets through which the product may be bought. The decision may be made because of special services required, *e.g.* television sets, or because of the need to create an appropriate prestige image, *e.g.* certain cosmetics available from chemists only.

(c) *Exclusive distribution.* This is a further development of selective distribution. Particular outlets are granted exclusive handling rights usually within prescribed geographical areas. Wholesalers are given exclusive distribution rights more frequently than retailers. Sometimes exclusive distribution or franchise rights are coupled with special financing arrangements for land, buildings or equipment, *e.g.* petrol station agreements.

50. Product characteristics. Those affecting channel decisions are as follows:

(a) *Frequency, value and quantity of purchases.* In general, low-value items bought in large quantity and frequently are widely distributed, using various channel combinations, whereas high-value items infrequently purchased are sold by selective or exclusive distribution, or direct to the consumer.

(b) *Value in relation to weight and density.* The usefulness of intermediaries in the case of large, heavy items of low unit value may lie in their provision of local storage and bulk breaking facilities.

(c) *Product life or seasonal demand.* Products which

deteriorate rapidly or are affected by seasonal demand involve special problems of risk and inventory control which have a bearing on channel selection. Speed of movement is essential and channels tend to be shorter. Special storage, *e.g.* refrigeration, or transport, *e.g.* air cargo, may be necessary.

(*d*) *Product service requirements*, *e.g.* repair facilities, spares.

51. Market characteristics. Those affecting channel decisions include the following:

(*a*) *Market size.* If the market is large the cost of performing all the marketing functions will probably be higher and manufacturers may prefer or be forced to use intermediaries extensively. Cost could be reduced, of course, by limiting geographical distribution.

(*b*) *Market structure.* Consumer markets are inevitably dispersed. There are, however, differences in the concentrations of the potential users and distributors of products. Industrial customers require services of different types, *e.g.* technical advice, ready availability of spare parts, and although they are fewer in number they may be widely scattered and have very different financial resources.

(*c*) *Market exposure.* Some products are bought almost on impulse and sales are affected by exhibitions and special displays. Others require much more personal selling.

52. Decisions connected with channel selection. After consideration of basic channel problems (**49, 50, 51**) manufacturers are faced with more specific problems such as the following:

(*a*) *Organisation of selective selling.* In most types of business there are many outlets but there is a disproportionate concentration of business in a small number of large units. This leads to "selective selling" and use of more than one channel, *e.g.* direct sales to large outlets, small outlets being supplied through wholesalers. Nevertheless, profitable operation may depend on securing wide distribution and/or promoting sales of slower-moving lines.

NOTE: Selective selling should not be confused with selective distribution (**49**(*b*)). By selective selling a manufacturer may succeed in obtaining intensive distribution.

(*b*) *Pricing structure.* (*See* V, **14, 15**.)

(*c*) *Terms of sale.* As distinct from price, special credit arrangements, guarantees, and arrangements for return of goods may be necessary.

(*d*) *Organisation of sales forces.* Sales forces may have to be organised partly by territory, partly by product type and partly by outlet size. Centralised buying has led to the creation of "special outlet sales managers" in many companies.

(*e*) *Promotional support.* Channel choice will determine to what extent advertising should be used to *pull* products through the channels and to what extent sales effort will be needed to *push* products through the channels (*see* VI, **9**). It may be necessary to supply private label brands (*see* VII, **21–23**).

(*f*) *Motivation and control of intermediaries.* Intermediaries are frequently order takers and problems of motivation and provision of sales training may arise. In selective or exclusive distribution systems it will be necessary to evaluate the performance of intermediaries following careful selection. Replacements will have to be considered from time to time. Both intermediaries and channels which are the most suitable or feasible in the early stages of development of a business may cease to be so later on. In general, the further the manufacturer is removed from the ultimate consumer by links in the channel chain, the more difficult it is for him to control the flow of goods.

PROGRESS TEST 9

1. What are the four main types of marketing institutions? **(2)**
2. What are the six basic processes in marketing? **(6)**
3. What are the main reasons for growth in mail order business? **(12)**
4. What are the advantages and disadvantages of the small independent retailer? **(15)**
5. Define supermarkets. **(17)**
6. What are the main general principles of chain store operations? **(21)**
7. What have been the main difficulties of retail co-operative societies in recent years? **(30)**
8. What are the main characteristics of discount stores? **(34)**
9. What services do wholesaler-sponsored voluntary groups offer? **(47)**
10. What is meant by "intensive," "selective" and "exclusive" distribution? **(49)**

CHAPTER X

SALES MANAGEMENT

SALES FORCES: TASKS AND ORGANISATION

1. The role of sales forces. Sales forces are concerned with some or all of the six basic steps of the sales process (*see* VI, **5**). The closing of the sale may be the most important contribution to the process which most salesmen make, but some may not be in a position to take orders, *e.g.* "detailmen" who call on hospitals and general medical practitioners to convey information about the products of pharmaceutical companies. The five other steps involve a salesman, however, in many activities. Amongst these are the following:

(*a*) He may provide display services, *e.g.* at grocery supermarkets.

(*b*) He may act mainly as a specialist adviser, *e.g.* on the installation of telecommunication systems.

(*c*) He may provide after-sales service and advice.

(*d*) He may actually deliver goods—van salesmen, bread roundsmen, etc.

(*e*) He may collect payment for goods delivered.

(*f*) He may be expected to advise on stock levels.

(*g*) He may train and motivate other salesmen, *e.g.* overseas agents, retail sales staff.

NOTE: Many salesmen are concerned with the sale of intangible services, *e.g.* insurance.

2. Selling and status. The range of products and services offered and the range of customer categories upon which salesmen might call are both enormous. Aircraft have to be sold to governments; milk has to be sold to housewives. Some products are bought repeatedly; others very infrequently.

The low status which attaches to the word "salesman" in Britain derives partly from a popular ignorance of the diversity of personal selling tasks. Companies often attempt to overcome the status problem by using job designations such as representative, technical consultant. This is unfortunate since all salesmen are concerned to a greater or lesser extent in actively persuading and educating prospective customers to reach the point of deciding to buy or to continue buying the company's products or services.

COMPANY OBJECTIVES AND SALES-FORCE DECISIONS

3. Sales force decisions. A company must decide why it is employing a sales force, what role the sales force is to perform in the marketing mix. This basic decision will affect other decisions:

(a) What is to be the size of the sales force?

(b) How should the sales force be organised; e.g. by products, by geographical territories, by customer categories?

(c) What is to be the comparative importance of the various activities of the sales force, e.g. actual selling, providing technical service, display?

(d) What kind of men (or women) are required?

(e) What levels and systems of payment should be adopted?

(f) What structure, e.g. levels of management, is required?

4. Sales force size. The size of the sales force will depend mainly on the following factors:

(a) *The resources available to the company* and consideration of returns in relation to alternative forms of investment at particular times under particular conditions. A company with small financial resources will clearly be restricted in employing salesmen, who inevitably carry a high burden of expense. A company may decide it can meet its objectives by other means, e.g. investment in advertising, and therefore may rely entirely on mail order selling.

(b) *The size of potential orders.* The expense of operation must be measured against the returns. It would, therefore, be logical to consider the minimum potential order size which would warrant the expense of personal representation.

(c) *The location and number of potential customers.* All other things being equal, consumer sales forces are larger than industrial sales forces since there are far more potential customers for consumer goods, scattered more evenly across wider areas. Industrial salesmen may, however, waste travelling time in visiting widely scattered accounts if too small a force is employed.

(d) *The buying habits and characteristics of potential customers.*

Existing efficient channels of distribution, *e.g.* good wholesalers and retailers, may mean that fewer salesmen are required. Lack of efficient channels and need for demonstrations and technical information—as in some industrial markets—may mean that the ratio of salesmen to potential end users should be high. The *frequency of call* rate must also be taken into account here.

(*e*) *The product and customer range.* Different products may sometimes be handled effectively by one salesman calling on similar types of outlets—or sometimes even on different types of outlets. The depth and breadth of product range may, however, lead to a position when salesmen become ineffective because they have too many products to handle or products which require different technical knowledge or sales journeys which are uneconomical.

(*f*) *Marketing policy.* The company may decide to concentrate on selective distribution or to attempt the widest possible distribution.

5. Sales force organisational patterns. Sales forces are normally organised on the basis of:

  (*a*) geographical areas;
  (*b*) product types;
  (*c*) customer types;
  (*d*) customer sizes; or
  (*e*) a combination of geography, product and customer product.

These five patterns are described in **6–10** below (*see* also **13**).

6. Allocation by geographical area. The possible advantages of a single salesman assigned to cover all company products in a particular territory are:

  (*a*) savings in travel expenses;
  (*b*) better local and customer knowledge;
  (*c*) avoidance of multiple calling on the same customer.

The products offered, however, must be fairly homogeneous and within the technical competence of the salesman to handle. In addition, the need for frequency of call must be judged against the number of calls which have to be made, when determining the extent of each salesman's area.

7. Allocation by product types. Sales force structures built around product specialisations have the advantage that

highly qualified salesmen can be employed to deal with
technical explanations and problems, *e.g.* pharmaceuticals,
lifting equipment. This type of structure is favoured by
larger companies who have highly diversified specialised
product lines, each making substantial profit contributions.

8. Allocation by customer types. Product specialisation
selling may lead to duplication of calling on the same customers,
whereas a specialised knowledge of different kinds of customers,
their organisations, attitudes and product applications, may
be just as important as a specialised knowledge of the product.
Sales forces may, therefore, be organised to call on particular
market segments, *e.g.* on laundries, on retail outlets.

9. Handling large outlets. The significance of large outlets
in relation to total market size has given rise to the practice
in some companies of creating a sales force to handle key
accounts. In some cases key accounts, often termed "House
Accounts," may be handled by the sales manager himself or
by other sales executives.

10. Mixed selling systems. A combination of the above
four basic types of structure is increasingly found in large
organisations offering diversified products to wide-ranging
markets. The combination approach leads to inter-company
communication problems, *e.g.* the relationship between product managers and sales managers. Not only is there a
staff-line organisation problem, but also a problem of co-
ordinating the objectives and plans of different product
managers competing for the attention of sales managers
responsible for the field selling operations.

The overall role of the sales force as a part of the promotion
sales process (*see* VII, **4**) must be determined in order that the
sales manager may be given a clear definition of his objectives
and the standards by which his performance will be judged.
The objectives will determine the responsibility and authority
assigned to him.

SALES MANAGEMENT TASKS

Sales management is concerned with the planning, direction
and control of sales forces. Objectives may differ, but there

are certain tasks common to almost all sales management roles.

11. Selection. Good selection presupposes a knowledge of the requirements of the particular job. It is, therefore, important that jobs should be analysed and that a detailed job description is available. The job description might lay down the overall objectives, detailed duties and responsibilities, limits of authority, organisational relationships and minimum standards of qualifications, experience and personal qualities required. Job analysis is necessary not only for selection but also for training, performance evaluation, and motivation.

Good selection also demands interviewing skill and a knowledge of personality, intelligence and aptitude tests which may guide judgment.

12. Training. New salesmen should be provided with a period of induction and organised training. Special refresher courses will be required from time to time, and there should be a continuous programme of planned development. Training is essentially the responsibility of line management and not of personnel departments who act in a "staff" capacity. Decisions have to be made on the length of training periods required, the content of the training (product knowledge, market knowledge, selling skills, administrative procedures, etc.) and the method. Method is extremely important and, as most training will be given on the job, it is important to select and train instructors.

13. Design of sales territories and allocation of salesmen. A sales territory may be part of a larger unit, *e.g.* a salesman's area which is part of a sales manager's district.

Basic considerations in designing sales territories are as follows:

    (*a*) To divide work loads equally.
    (*b*) To provide adequate sales potential for motivation purposes.
    (*c*) To reduce travel and expense as much as possible.
    (*d*) To provide for simple administration and control.

The establishment of sales potential in a given area provides a basis against which performance can be assessed, but it is often more difficult to achieve sales in some areas than in others. Again, a sales manager may decide that, even if it were possible to equalise opportunities to sell, some inequality should be preserved to allow for the introduction of new men and means of motivating more highly skilled or more senior men. The problems of territory design and allocation are linked inextricably with the problems of target setting and reward (*see* **14**).

Once a territory is defined it is important to consider how best coverage may be achieved and routeing plans in relation to the salesman's home base can make enormous differences to operating efficiency.

14. Allocation of targets and financial considerations. Salesmen are paid in three main ways:

(a) *Payment by straight salary.* This method is commonly used in sales situations either where the role of the salesman involves many considerations other than actual orders received, or when orders are very infrequent, *e.g.* in many industrial markets. The method does not, of course, preclude the setting of targets as indirect non-financial motivation.

(b) *Payment by salary and commission or bonus.* This method is to be found regularly in sales situations where orders are frequently taken or credited to salesmen, *e.g.* in consumer products or industrial materials.

(c) *Payment by straight commission.* This method is increasingly rare and is normally associated with speciality selling, *e.g.* of encyclopaedias or specialised capital equipment by agents.

Financial incentives have a very profound effect on the performance of sales forces, but they must be devised in such a way that the additional payments are geared to an appropriate increase in company profitability and so that the basis on which rewards are given is seen to be as fair as possible. The sales manager, therefore, has a considerable problem in taking a complete sales target and allocating it among individual areas and territories.

While individual financial incentives are considered by many to be the most effective, it is often impracticable to allocate the reward for a particular sale to one specific salesman. One man may have taken a central order, others may have provided displays, others may have provided technical services. *Group bonus schemes* are, therefore, sometimes applied to areas or districts. It is sometimes argued that the group bonus has other advantages over individual incentives in developing the group spirit which is necessary for more effective total sales performance.

Under purely commission systems of payment the company loses direct control and unless commissions are based on very sophisticated lines it is difficult to develop business systematically, *e.g.* by introducing new accounts, or by spreading sales across products or customer types. Once established, it is difficult to adjust commission rates; sales targets and bonus systems to salaried sales forces require regular revision.

15. Fixed and variable elements in financial rewards. Salesmen often enjoy a number of fringe benefits which, unlike bonuses, become a fixed cost. These benefits may include provision of a company car with special concessions for private motoring, or an allowance for mileage for use of a personally owned car, garage allowances, lunch allowances, safe driving rewards, entertainment expenses and so on. The problem is to determine compensation in the light of the task to be performed, the supply of suitable men, the conditions in the particular country, and practices of competitors. This includes:

(*a*) the system of compensation;
(*b*) the level of compensation; and
(*c*) the constituent parts of the total compensation.

Few generalisations are of any value, but, where actual selling is a frequently performed and major role of the salesman, a combination of fixed and variable compensation elements seems to be ideal. The fixed element has to be sufficiently high to provide for basic security and living standards; the variable element has to be sufficiently meaningful to both salesman and company. A combination of fixed and variable remuneration has advantages in adjusting potential earnings according to changes in costs of living, changes in the company's profit record and various combinations of seniority and selling achievement. The problems are to devise equitable systems and to set equitable targets.

16. Direction and control. Important factors are as follows:

(a) *Economy in the use of time and effort.* The maximum amount of time should be spent on the outlets of major profit to the company. Waiting and travelling time should be kept to the minimum.

(b) *Arranging call frequency and rating.* Some outlets will require longer or more regular calls than others.

(c) *Development of business.* This includes increasing the business transacted with existing customers as well as locating and opening new accounts.

(d) *Reporting.* Reports will be required daily, weekly or monthly on calls made. Salesmen should also learn to report back significant field intelligence, *e.g.* competitive activity, future developments by major customers. Reports on lost business or complaints will be required.

(e) *Evaluating the performance of salesmen.* Salesmen's performance should be evaluated on quantitative factors, *e.g.* progress towards targets, comparison with past performance, business development in relation to territory potential. Qualitative assessment will also be necessary since the salesman will have to undertake part of the selling process other than closing sales (*see* VI, **5**).

MOTIVATION

17. Special problems of motivating salesmen. Motivation of field sales forces provides special problems, for the following reasons:

(a) A salesman meets frustration very regularly—every time he fails to make a sale or gain a favourable buying reaction. He can quickly lose confidence and his future performance suffers.

(b) A salesman works alone and lacks the immediate moral support of company colleagues. Sometimes he feels he lacks company backing if deliveries are late or invoices are incorrectly made out.

(c) A salesman has irregular hours and sometimes is away from home. This may lead to special personal tensions.

(d) Few people are always self-motivating and high morale and a sense of reward or achievement are necessary for a man to sustain effort if left entirely to his own devices.

18. Means of motivation. The need for a favourable

working climate is, therefore, obvious. This can be stimulated in various ways:

(a) By providing helpful direction, *e.g.* assistance in field operations, by personal visits rather than perpetual written communications.

(b) By arranging sales and social meetings periodically.

(c) By arranging special sales contests.

(d) By making special efforts in writing and by telephone to keep men in the picture about company or area developments and progress.

(e) By encouraging positive suggestions for improved personal or company operation.

(f) By devising fair performance evaluation schemes, assisting men to develop their own capabilities, and providing a route to promotion or increased financial reward.

(g) By reducing unnecessary administrative procedures.

(h) By providing equipment and information to assist in the selling operation, *e.g.* sales manuals, sales literature, samples, demonstration models.

SALES FORECASTING

19. Sales forecasting and sales targets. In Chapter VIII attention was drawn to the fundamental bases of control, *viz.* sales targets and budgets. Sales targets are derived from a consideration of sales forecasts, *i.e.* levels of sales anticipated at various levels of marketing expense. Sales targets do not necessarily coincide exactly with the finally accepted forecast since targets are motivational tools (**14**) and may be set at a slightly higher level than the forecast in order to stimulate salesmen to greater effort. Since sales targets are, however, derived from forecasts it is now appropriate to examine forecasting methods and procedures.

20. Basic forecasting considerations. Sales forecasting methods and procedures vary very considerably from company to company but there are really three basic considerations to be taken into account:

(a) The general economic environment and outlook.

(b) The particular industry environment and outlook.

(c) The outlook for the particular company and its products.

(d) Company and competitive marketing plans.

21. Forecasting time periods. Forecasts cover different time periods:

(a) *Short-term.* The operating budget forecast covers the immediate financial year and is used to determine standard costs, prices, cash flow and similar matters.

(b) *Long-term.* Forecasts are required for varying periods of time ahead, to provide for items such as major capital requirement, new market or product developments.

22. Basic forecasting methods. Three basic methods are used for short-term forecasts—often in combination:

(a) Estimates (or guesses) by sales managers.

(b) Internal analysis of company data, *e.g.* using regression analysis (*see* V, **24**).

(c) Analysis of company data related to other external performance criteria, *e.g.* economic conditions, industry trends. This form of analysis normally involves the use of statistical techniques such as correlation analysis (*see* V, **24**).

23. Sources of additional forecasting information. In order to supplement the information gained from various forms of statistical analysis, companies sometimes undertake the following exercises:

(a) *Surveys of buyers' intentions.* It would obviously be impracticable to approach every potential buyer or even to identify every one. Consequently a sample is normally taken (*see* III, **18–25**). Enquiries may be carried out by market research personnel, but sometimes sales forces are asked to co-operate. This method is more often practised when there is a comparatively small number of significant purchasers, *e.g.* in some industrial markets. Difficulties arise if:

(*i*) buyers are unwilling to give information (salesmen may find this a major problem);

(*ii*) buyers give deliberately false information;

(*iii*) buyers themselves don't really know.

(b) *Seeking the opinion of salesmen and sales executives.* The advantages could be:

(*i*) that men in touch with actual buying conditions should know what is likely to happen;

(*ii*) that the forecasts will be readily available by products or areas;

(*iii*) that the sales force will support the forecast more readily because it has participated in the process.

F

This practice also has its greatest validity in highly technical selling fields. Adjustments have to be made to compensate for the over-optimism of some salesmen and the low estimates of others who fear that targets will be increased if sales estimate are high.

24. Problems in the analysis of internal data. Analysis of company data should take into consideration the following:

(a) Variations in demand—resulting from seasonal factors, cyclical changes in consumption and cyclical changes in inventory.

(b) Secular change—long-term trends of growth or decline in demand brought about by substitution or obsolescence.

(c) Random factors—chance or temporary changes in sales.

(d) Changes in the company's own market share position.

25. Statistical processes. Once seasonal factors are removed, random factors can be eliminated by the use of moving averages to produce a trend line (*see* NOTE (*i*) below). The problem now is to project the trend. Sometimes statistical means are used, *e.g.* the use of the *least–squares method*, (*see* NOTE (*ii*) below). There still remains the problem of allowing for changes in the business cycle which affect some types of industry (*e.g.* textiles) more than others (*e.g.* food). Sometimes it is possible to use *correlation analysis*, *i.e.* to establish a relationship between specific materials or products, and demand for a company's own products. Thus a change in demand for retail products may be seen to have direct relationship with a change in demand for packaging, or a change in population with *per capita* demand for food.

NOTE:

(*i*) A moving average is a moving total divided by the number of periods constituting that total. A moving total for twelve-monthly periods, for example, would be determined by dropping out the earliest monthly total and substituting the latest monthly total as it becomes available.

(*ii*) It is most unlikely that the figures to be plotted on a graph will fall in a straight line which would show immediately the trend. The trend has, therefore, to be established by finding the line which would most nearly fit, *i.e.* where the values shown on the line (the trend) would be nearer to actual values than any other line. The method of least

squares is based on the mathematical concept that the best
line is the one that minimises the total of the squared
deviations.

26. Forecasting accuracy. The extent of forecasting error
should be considered in the light of the cost of excessive stock
holding or out of stock situations and delivery hold-ups. It
may not be economically justifiable to incur the cost of
reducing errors by plus or minus 1 per cent, but it is certainly
important to know the likely limits of error and few companies are really satisfied with the reliability of their present
forecasting procedures. If inaccuracy is seriously affecting
profits, greater attention must be paid to preparing the basic
economic assumptions, securing relevant and reliable data
and applying sound statistical techniques, and to analysing
more closely the effect on demand of product policy, pricing
and promotion.

PROGRESS TEST 10

1. What are the various functions which might be performed
by sales forces? **(1)**
2. What considerations might determine the size of a sales
force? **(4)**
3. On what bases might sales forces be organised? **(5)**
4. What are the problems of providing financial incentives to
sales forces? **(14, 15)**
5. How might salesmen be motivated? **(18)**
6. What are the problems in interpreting company data for the
purpose of forecasting? **(24)**

CHAPTER XI

MARKETING INDUSTRIAL GOODS AND SERVICES

The main principles of marketing as set out in earlier chapters apply to the marketing of all types of goods and services. The special characteristics of industrial markets, however, lead to special problems in the application of those principles.

BASIC MARKET CHARACTERISTICS

1. Definition. Industrial goods and services are those bought by manufacturers, distributors, institutions (*e.g.* schools, government departments, extractive industries, agriculture and other commercial enterprises) for their own use rather than for resale.

2. Classification. There are four basic categories as follows:

(*a*) *Capital goods.* These goods include such items as factory structures, machinery, office furniture and materials handling equipment. Capital goods are treated by accountants as capital assets of a business, their value being depreciated over given periods of time.

(*b*) *Components and materials.* These include basic raw materials and partly or wholly processed materials and goods which form ultimately part of the products which are sold to customers, *e.g.* copper, tyres, sparking plugs, packaging.

(*c*) *Supplies.* Supplies are goods which assist production and distribution but are not included in finished products and, unlike capital goods, are not regarded as a capital investment. Examples include lubricating oils, stationery, cleaning materials.

(*d*) *Business services.* These cover a wide range of intangible services, *e.g.* business consultancy, office cleaning, advertising.

3. Special features of industrial products. There are certain common features distinguishing industrial and consumer products as follows:

(a) *Product similarity.* Industrial products have frequently to conform with national or international standards. This limits the extent to which a producer can differentiate his products from those of competitors. Again, buyers often lay down their own specifications. In general, the more a product is processed or fabricated the greater is the possibility of differentiation: *cf.* steel and office furniture.

(b) *Technical complexity.* Many industrial products call for a high level of technological skill and precision, *e.g.* electric motors, paper-making machinery. This factor means that not only is there often a need to maintain high investment in research and development activities and manufacturing processing, but it is frequently essential to supply technical assistance and advice. Provision for after-sales maintenance and for the supplying of spare parts is also frequently necessary.

(c) *High unit values.* Industrial goods, *e.g.* capital equipment, are frequently highly expensive items. The unit value of components and materials may be comparatively low, but the quantity required usually means that the value of total sales to individual customers is high.

(d) *Irregularity of purchase.* Materials which are used as part of finished products must be bought fairly regularly, but many other items, *e.g.* equipment, have a long working life and their purchase can be deferred. Components and materials are also frequently bought on a contract basis and the opportunity to obtain new business may arise infrequently.

4. Special features of industrial patterns. The following considerations are particularly important:

(a) *Derived demand.* The demand for industrial products is dependent on the demand for consumer products. A fall in consumer demand would quickly affect the demand for materials used in consumer goods, and a lack of buoyancy in consumer markets would lead to reluctance on the part of producers to buy new equipment or replace existing equipment. Because of derived demand, industrial markets are subject to greater irregularities in demand pattern than consumer markets and the problems of forecasting are greater. Not only are there annual fluctuations; demand levels also often vary enormously from month to month.

(b) *Inelasticity of demand.* From the above it will be seen that lowering prices cannot be expected to have the same effect as in many consumer markets. If there is no ultimate consumer demand the price of industrial goods and services is irrelevant. On the other hand, if there is a lowering in total demand, price reduction might provide an important advantage in the case of an individual company. Nevertheless, large price differences are unlikely since producers will be often using similar materials from similar sources and competitors will probably react by reducing their prices. The greatest price fluctuations are to be found in markets for materials and components, where there are more suppliers competing for business than in capital goods markets.

5. Special features of industrial market structures. There are a number of marked structural characteristics of industrial markets. The most important are as follows:

(a) *Number of potential buyers.* It is clear that there are fewer potential industrial than consumer buyers. These buyers also have more specialised needs. Thus industrial markets consist of a number of special segments. The demand for certain products will be limited to one specialised segment, *e.g.* agricultural machinery. The demand for other products may be spread across a number of segments, *e.g.* industrial oils. The total number of potential buyers in different segments will vary tremendously: *cf.* distributive services and aircraft manufacture. In all industrial market segments, however, a small number of buyers account for a very high percentage of the total market demand.

(b) *Geographical concentration.* Many industries are concentrated in particular geographical areas, *e.g.* paper making, car manufacture. On the other hand, the demand for certain products and services is geographically widespread, *e.g.* industrial cleaning materials.

6. Special features of industrial buying. Attention must be drawn to the following:

(a) Economic motives (*see* 7).
(b) The group-buying influence (*see* 8).
(c) Professionalism (*see* 9).
(d) Reciprocal buying (*see* 10).
(e) Supplier loyalty (*see* 11).

7. Economic motives. Industrial buyers are essentially concerned with the acquisition of goods and services which will provide measurable benefits in terms of ultimate profit. This, combined with the fact that the cost of purchase is often high, means that rational economic motives are much more significant than purely emotional considerations.

Although industrial products are bought on a performance and benefit basis, however, it should be remembered that industrial buyers are subject to human emotions. Emotional aspects of buying may be seen, for example, in the following:

(a) Differences in attitudes of buyers towards features such as colour and design which may have no obvious economic value.

(b) Differences in attitudes of buyers towards particular salesmen, sales literature, supplying companies.

(c) Differences in attitude towards salesmen in general which may have a sociological or psychological basis. The position and status of a professional buyer in the formal organisation structure, for example, will affect his attitude to sales approaches. One buyer with low company status may wish to bolster his ego by adopting a militant manner to salesmen; another may be anxious to learn of new developments in order to gain a benefit for his company which might improve his own standing.

8. The group-buying influence. The final purchasing order for industrial goods and services may be signed by one man, but the decision to buy is usually the result of the opinions of a number of people. These people may be motivated in different ways. The benefits seen by a manufacturing specialist may be minimised by an accounting specialist for example. Again, persons who influence the buying decision may have different formal and informal status in their organisations. In general, research has shown that, the larger the organisation, the greater the number of people there are who influence buying decisions.

9. Professionalism. Industrial buyers are often not only familiar with technical and basic cost requirements; they may be specialists in such matters as evaluating sources of supply and deciding on the appropriate level of investment in stocks. Buying organisations are more and more concerned with setting basic standards of product and delivery performance, service requirements and so on which must be met before a potential supplier can be seriously considered. The level of buying expertise varies tremendously. In general, the larger the buying company and the greater the expenditure involved, either in terms of capital equipment or in terms of cost of materials and components in relation to total costs, the greater is the professionalism of the actual buyer.

10. Reciprocal buying. This may be an informal arrangement whereby a buying organisation tends to favour suppliers who are customers. On the other hand, there may be strictly formal agreements. Formal agreements are not particularly widespread and have the great disadvantage of preventing buyers from obtaining the best value. It should here be pointed out that many large industrial organisations have highly diversified interests in different types of businesses. Sometimes there is complete control of capital; at other times there is a considerable percentage share-holding. Formal and informal reciprocal or transfer buying arrangements might be anticipated in such circumstances. Transfer arrangements apply to systems whereby one company or department buys components or processed materials from another, each unit operating as a profit centre. Sometimes when transfer arrangements are possible, buyers are still free to obtain supplies from outside sources if there are special advantages.

11. Supplier loyalty. Among industrial buyers there is frequently much greater loyalty to traditional suppliers than is the case in consumer markets. The reasons may be essentially emotional, *e.g.* the establishment of a personal relationship between buyers and sellers. Another important reason is that a new piece of equipment or new materials in industrial processes frequently affect total performance. Industrial buyers are, therefore, reluctant to change. Large organisations may have research and pilot plant facilities where prolonged testing can be carried out and the period of negotiation for a major purchase may be quite prolonged.

SPECIAL FEATURES OF THE MARKETING MIX

12. Industrial selling. Direct selling, *i.e.* from producer to user, is a feature of many industrial marketing operations. The main reasons for this shortening of the channels of distribution are as follows:

(*a*) There are fewer customers and these may be geographically concentrated. The potential size of orders is large. Thus fewer salesmen are necessary to establish direct contact and the cost in relation to potential business is normally lower than in the case of direct personal selling to domestic customers.

(b) Considerable technical knowledge and demonstrations may be required in the selling process. The manufacturer's salesmen can be expected to be more effective, therefore, than salesmen of intermediaries who may handle a wide range of products.

(c) Many industrial items are bought to individual specifications and involve direct negotiation between buyer and seller on a technical level.

(d) Items of high unit value may require special credit arrangements which are more easily negotiated on a direct basis. Some items may be leased or rented.

(e) The importance of servicing and after-sales technical advice leads many buyers to prefer direct dealings with manufacturers.

(f) Industrial buyers need a much more individual approach than that of consumer buyers. It would be impossible in most cases to arrange for a standard monthly presentation of a drive brand, for example. Individual benefits have to be sold to meet the needs of particular organisations and people within those organisations.

NOTE: It is important that industrial salesmen should combine appropriate technical expertise and selling skill. There is a danger that industrial salesmen may be appointed on the basis of the technical qualifications alone and there is frequently insufficient training in selling skills provided.

13. Industrial advertising. Advertising is a much smaller constituent of marketing costs than in consumer marketing. Apart from the fact that advertising budgets are lower, there are many distinguishing features of industrial promotion, including those considered in **14–17** below.

14. Use of mass media. As industrial markets are highly segmented it is usually wasteful to use mass media. Some companies do advertise in the national press for the following reasons:

(a) To build up a corporate image of a large progressive organisation. Large companies whose products may be used in many market segments, e.g. I.C.I., are more likely to derive direct advantage from mass communication media than smaller companies offering a limited product range. Corporate images also serve to attract investment and personnel.

(b) To attract the attention of executives who may influence the buying decision but rarely have the opportunity or inclination to read specialised journals.

(c) To stimulate consumer demand for products which will reflect on industrial demand. Consumer campaigns for man-made fibres and plastics are good examples of this. The industrial manufacturer may have much greater resources than the distributors along the distribution chain. In some cases, therefore, industrial manufacturers bear the whole cost of such advertising; in other they may make a contribution towards the cost of advertising.

NOTE: Consumer campaigns organised by industrial manufacturers are often associated with branding, *e.g.* Terylene, Acrilan.

15. Specialised media. Industrial advertising is usually concentrated in the following media:

(a) *Trade press.* The range of journals is extremely wide; some are aimed at highly specialised readers, *e.g. Photographic Abstracts*, while others have a more general appeal, *e.g. Purchasing*. There are also considerable variations in costs of space, frequency of publication, circulation (often an estimate and not subjected to audit) and so on. This leads to specially acute problems in media scheduling and planning.

(b) *Business and professional journals.* These are ever changing in number, format, circulation and influence. Professional journals often have a guaranteed circulation to members, *e.g. Work Study, Marketing*.

(c) *Direct mail.* There is evidence of the growing use of planned direct mail campaigns. In many industrial markets where prospective customers can be identified, are relatively few in number, and can be mailed at different times, use of this medium can bring valuable results, *e.g.* in stimulating enquiries to be followed up by salesmen; in keeping companies constantly informed of developments between sales visits.

(d) *Films.* Expenditure on documentary films for cinema showing could be justified by very few companies, but the specialised use of films is particularly appropriate in industrial markets. Industrial products are often large and difficult to demonstrate, specially if complex industrial processes are involved. Films can be used at trade shows, at national and international exhibitions, and at private company demonstrations. The use of special equipment for the showing of films by salesmen on customer calls should lead to the stimulation of greater attention and interest.

(e) *Sales aids.* The provision of catalogues, price lists and sales literature is a vital part of any industrial advertising programme. Insufficient attention is often paid to the design and use of this material and salesmen are inclined to rely too much on verbal descriptions and means of persuasion.

(f) *Exhibitions.* These are a feature of industrial marketing, but the large investment involved in participating in many national exhibitions is often unjustified except on the basis of keeping in line with competition. The case for arranging mobile exhibitions, *e.g.* in vans and special trains, is usually much stronger, as is that for participating in important international exhibitions (*see* XII, **55**).

16. Advertising agencies. Large agencies often concentrate on consumer goods campaigns because of the higher total expenditure and often better media discounts (15% as opposed to 10% offered by many trade publications). There are sometimes, therefore, difficulties in finding agencies willing and able to undertake campaigns suitably geared to industrial users. Some smaller agencies specialise in this kind of work.

17. Establishing advertising objectives. Because of the range of specialised needs and buying motivations and the relative infrequency of buying, it is more difficult to establish clear objectives for a promotional programme than in consumer markets. The relatively low budgets and wide range of media available complicate the issue and advertising expenditure is frequently wasted. It is particularly important that objectives should be clarified when resources are so scarce. Too many industrial advertisements attempt to communicate too much at one time and too many campaigns are spoilt by attempting wide coverage at infrequent intervals.

NOTE: Publicity (*see* VII, **33**) is a specially powerful industrial marketing tool.

18. Conclusion. The total value of industrial goods and services bought in the United Kingdom exceeds the total value of consumers' expenditure. This fact together with the special complexities of industrial marketing covered above should emphasise the importance of the adoption of the marketing philosophy by all companies involved. Yet the process of change from production orientation to marketing orientation is slow. Vast sums are being spent on research and development of products while the amount of money invested in analysis of the markets to be supplied is infinitessimal.

PROGRESS TEST 11

1. Industrial markets are varied and complex. How might they be clarified in order to examine broadly common characteristics of purchasing behaviour? (**2**(*a*)–(*d*))

2. What is the special significance of demand elasticity in industrial marketing? (**4**(*a*), (*b*))

3. What are the special features affecting the industrial buying process which create selling problems quite different from those usually encountered in selling consumer products? (**6**(*a*)–(*d*))

4. Why is "direct selling" such an important factor in many industrial markets? (**12**(*a*)–(*f*))

5. What are the special difficulties in devising advertising campaigns for industrial goods and services? (**13–17**)

CHAPTER XII

INTERNATIONAL MARKETING

THE SIGNIFICANCE OF INTERNATIONAL TRADE

1. The principles of comparative advantage. There is nothing new in the notion of inter-nation marketing. The *theory of comparative advantage* derives from the idea that nations will tend to capitalise on the possession of special natural resources or special skills, so that they can offer to other nations advantages in terms of price or special product qualities. They will import products which they themselves cannot produce as economically or as well. The theory is complicated in practice by shifting variables—wage levels, material costs, transportation costs, production methods and costs, scientific and technological development, educational standards and so on. In addition, financial and legal problems complicate the issue and various restrictions of free trade are imposed by governments. Again, there is a natural tendency to satisfy an unsaturated home demand before entering international markets.

2. The balance of trade. Nations lacking essential materials are compelled to import and must attempt to balance their trade by exporting.

The United Kingdom, lacking valuable raw materials and being highly industrialised, is particularly dependent on international trade. To maintain a balance of trade it is necessary to earn sufficient from visible and invisible exports to meet international obligations and finance imports and the outflow of capital.

3. Recent trends in international trade. The factors which have led to an accelerating rate of change in the pattern of international business are as follows:

(*a*) Social and economic factors (*see* **4**).
(*b*) Technological factors (*see* **5**).

(c) Legal and political factors (*see* **6**).

These factors are, of course, interacting.

4. Social and economic factors (*see* I, **3**).   Amongst major considerations are the following:

(a) Industrialisation.
(b) Education.
(c) Distribution of wealth.
(d) Life expectation.
(e) Population size.
(f) Social and physical mobility (*see* I, **3**(c), (d)).
(g) Urbanisation.
(h) The development of economic trading blocs (*see* **6**(d)).

5. Technological factors.   Changes are taking place almost at an exponential rate.   Examples are very evident: the use of atomic power in generating electricity, the increased speed of air transport, automation and increasing mechanisation in industrial processes.   International trade in manufactured products is increasing at a greater rate than trade in primary commodities.   The need for primary commodities, however, does not increase in direct proportion to the growth of population or income.   Countries which are industrialised tend to trade with one another more and more and so the gap between the economic development of industrially developed and non-developed countries tends to intensify.   More and more countries are becoming industrialised, however, and seek to develop their economies by international exchange.   Even those countries which are comparatively self-contained, *e.g.* the USA, are increasingly involved in international marketing.

6. Legal and political factors.   National and international bodies have been working towards the removal of economic and financial barriers.   Examples can be seen in the following:

(a) *The General Agreement on Tariffs and Trade* (GATT). This agreement, signed by some 50 countries in 1948, is aimed at lowering trade barriers.·   Most industrialised countries except the USSR and China are members.
(b) *The International Monetary Fund.* This organisation was set up in 1945 to assist in overcoming currency problems,

e.g. the maintenance of parity amongst currencies and the correction of temporary shortages of particular currencies.

(*c*) *The Organisation for Economic Co-operation and Development.* This organisation was set up in 1961 with a membership of twenty countries including the United States and Great Britain. Its aim is to foster the growth of the national income of its members through co-operation.

(*d*) *Economic trading groups.* One of the prime aims of these groups is to remove trade restrictions (*e.g.* tariffs, quotas) amongst members. The European Economic Community comprising France, West Germany, Italy, Belgium, the Netherlands and Luxembourg was set up by the Treaty of Rome in 1957; completely free trade was achieved in July 1968. The European Free Trade Association comprising the UK, Norway, Sweden, Denmark, Austria, Portugal and Switzerland was formed in 1959. Other groups are emerging, *e.g.* in South-East Asia, Latin America, Africa. At the same time there are the centrally planned economies of groups of communist countries with external selling and buying conducted by state agencies.

(*e*) *Various forms of assistance* provided to exporters by national governments.

7. Significance of recent trends. As a consequence of these changes truly multi-national companies are developing. Multi-national companies may be defined as those which have manufacturing or other substantial investment overseas and which make management decisions on the basis of global opportunities and global resources. Few companies have reached this situation but many have found the need to effect economies of scale and by doing so have become more dependent on world markets; others have realised the increasing global opportunities now being opened up.

THE POSITION OF THE UK

8. Productivity and international trade expansion. Britain's share of an increasing volume of world trade is falling. The decline is more marked in some industrial groups than others—notably in the more traditional industries, *e.g.* textiles.

Various reasons may be advanced, but all amount really to a failure to maintain a marketing advantage in increasingly competitive conditions. Sellers' markets have almost invariably become *buyers'* markets and, where attention has been paid to the specific needs of customers, companies and industries have been relatively successful, *e.g.* those that manufacture specialised paints, high-quality woollen goods, sports cars. Often exports have been increased in spite of pricing disadvantages. In general, however, the prices of German, Japanese and Italian goods have not risen so sharply as those of British goods. It could be argued that the Japanese have had the advantages of lower labour costs, but a similar argument is not completely true of Germany. Where price advantages have been gained by Germany, Italy, France and Japan, they have been achieved by marked improvements in productivity rather than by simple differences in wage rates. Improvements in productivity have been matched by, and to a large extent made possible by, aggressive overseas marketing and a philosophy of global growth.

9. Changes in demand patterns, markets and products. Apart from considerations of prices, productivity, and increasing competition, it is clear that many of Britain's traditional markets have become self-sufficient and, indeed, are exporting some products in competition with Britain. It is also evident that world demand for the kind of products on which British international trade was mainly dependent before the Second World War had declined, or expanded at a much slower rate than the demand for other types of products. It may be argued that government policy often aimed at damping down home consumption to stimulate exports in post-war years has had a dampening effect on industrial activity. It does not follow that a restriction of spending power in home markets will lead to increased attention on the part of manufacturers to export business. Home and overseas business are not mutually exclusive and a healthy home market may well be a condition for competitive overseas operations— and in some cases, unless trade barriers are erected, a condition for survival at home.

10. Major opportunities for British trade. The greatest opportunities for British exports in the near future would appear to be in three areas, *viz.* Western Europe, the USA and the Commonwealth. It is the more highly industrialised countries which generate the highest level of world trade and these countries lie within the areas specified, with the exception of communist countries. Communist countries are relaxing controls to some extent and limited opportunities for trade exist. These may be particularly important for certain industries and companies, but East-West trade represented only 4·5% of the world total in 1966 as compared with 16% generated by the USA and 18% by countries within the European Economic Community.

11. Analysing opportunities in world markets. It is likely that success or failure in world markets will depend more on marketing expertise than on manufacturing or financial resources. The first consideration is to discover what the market wants and is likely to buy. It is therefore necessary to obtain the following basic information:

(a) *Population details:*
  (i) Total population.
  (ii) Growth rate.
  (iii) Geographical concentrations.
  (iv) Income levels, distribution and trends.
  (v) Consumption trends.
  (vi) Family size and number of households—solidity of family groupings.
  (vii) Language, religious, cultural and social groupings—buying patterns and attitudes.
  (viii) Educational standards.

(b) *Economic resources:*
  (i) The existing structure of economic wealth—minerals, agriculture, manufacturing.
  (ii) Likely changes in the economic structure and rate of change.

(c) *Communications:* Availability and cost of transport to and in the overseas territory—road systems, ports facilities, railways, airports, telephones, etc.

(d) *Location, climate and topography:* Possible effects on resources and productivity.

(e) *Government policy and political philosophy:*
  (i) Attitude to foreign trade and investment.
  (ii) Taxation policy.
  (iii) Economic planning and control; attitude towards particular products or industrial development.
  (iv) Foreign exchange policy.
  (v) Military demands on economic resources.

12. World demand: basic systems. Analysis of world markets on the above lines will reveal certain basic similarities and differences arising from basic systems, *viz.* sociâl, economic, technical, political and legal.

13. The social system. Nations develop social attitudes and customs which derive from their peculiar pattern of cultural development. Attitudes towards the family, social class structure, class mobility and material values, for example, have a basis in the moral and ethical standards of a community, standards often rooted in religious beliefs. Some of the effects on social systems caused by very different religions, *e.g.* Hinduism and Christianity, will be obvious; other attitudes, *e.g.* those towards colour, require close investigation. Significant differences in attitudes and customs are to be found in Christian countries. Attitudes towards certain products and advertising copy are quite different in France from those in Holland.

It should be noted that attitudes and beliefs tend to strengthen over time and thus countries are often associated or associate themselves with special abilities or characteristics. The German, for example, considers himself technically superior but is prepared to buy a Ford car combining German technical achievement and American styling. "Image" associated with particular countries persits long after the basis for the "image" has disappeared. It is, therefore, more difficult to remove a reputation for poor delivery service than to create it. Changes can be affected, however. The Japanese reputation for shoddy workmanship is fast disappearing, but only as a result of aggressive marketing.

14. The economic system. Differences in market opportunities are frequently the result of differences in the following:

    (*a*) Standards of living.
    (*b*) Costs of labour, materials, capital and equipment.
    (*c*) Rate of population growth.
    (*d*) Distribution methods.
    (*e*) Spread of industrialisation.
    (*f*) Availability of credit.
    (*g*) Communications.

Market similarities spring from economic similarities, the influence of mass consumption societies, international companies and international advertising. Patterns of consumption and income distribution follow similar trends according to broadly defined stages of economic development. The pyramid pattern of income distribution with wealth concentrated in a few hands moves through various stages until an ovoid pattern denotes a high level of industrialisation with incomes of the majority narrowly differentiated and well above subsistence level. Thus countries with a high *per capita* income level have an ever-increasing demand for consumer luxury goods while the demand for necessities remains fairly stable. The difference lies in the type of luxuries, *e.g.* telephones, refrigerators, washing machines, cars.

15. The technical system. The development of technology depends on economic factors, *e.g.* the availability of capital and professional and skilled labour, and on political factors, *e.g.* high investment in defence projects as in the USA. One of the major problems is that the "technological gap," the difference in technical knowledge and its application, is widening as a result of these economic and political factors (*see* **4, 6, 11** above).

16. The political and legal system. Political philosophies and government actions based on these philosophies affect the pattern of international trade. Moves towards liberalisation have been mentioned earlier (**6**), but amongst major differences are the following:

(*a*) The extent of state intervention in the control of the economy, *e.g.* complete state control in communist countries, national planning as in France.

(*b*) The attitude of governments, *e.g.* towards the import and export of goods and currency, the investment of foreign capital, the use of foreign labour.

(*c*) Political stability. Frequent changes in government, *e.g.* in Latin America, give rise to economic and financial instability.

(*d*) Business law and legislative procedures.

(*e*) Efficiency and integrity of civil servants.

17. Distribution patterns. The major differences between distribution patterns in various countries are due to the following factors:

(a) Economic factors (*see* **18**).
(b) Social factors (*see* **19**).
(c) Geographical and communication factors (*see* **20**).

18. Economic factors.

(a) *Ownership.* In communist countries, for example, there is complete state control of the distribution process. In some other areas state-owned enterprises or co-operatives co-exist with private institutions.

(b) *Number, physical size and turnover of retail outlets.* In general, the more developed economically a country is, the larger is the size and turnover of major retail and wholesale outlets. Average retail store sales in the USA are thirty-five times higher than in India, for example.

(c) *Functions performed and services offered.* Self-service, for example, is a feature of more highly developed Western economies. Other differences occur in the provision of credit, after-sales service, stock-holding and risk-carrying, promotional and display facilities. These activities may require financial support from manufacturers or wholesalers where retailers are notably short of capital.

(d) *Assortment of products.* In general, the less developed the economy the greater the degree of specialisation in channels.

(e) *Productivity and manpower.* In more highly developed countries great attention is being paid to the economies of operation. This may lead to lower margins and a decline in personal service.

(f) *Industrial product distribution.* Where there is a lack of industrialisation, industrial goods are frequently handled by importers who carry a wide range of products. This presents difficulties in providing for technically competent after-sales service.

19. Social factors.

(a) In many countries manufacturing is considered to be more socially useful than distribution. The low status of wholesaling in many underdeveloped countries has, for example, led to the dominance of distribution by immigrant populations.

(b) In all countries various types of outlets have greater appeal for particular strata of society than for others.

(c) There are considerable differences in the extent to which buying is regarded as a social activity by both industrial and domestic customers.

20. Geographical and communication factors. In a large country with a comparatively underdeveloped economy and

communication system, historical trading patterns and disper-
sion of customers may lead to a greater number of links in the
distribution chain. One of the problems in this kind of
situation is that there is often a marked difference in attitudes
and objectives of traders in the distribution chain. Lack of
advertising media intensifies the problem.

METHODS OF EXPORTING

Once a company has decided to enter overseas markets it
has to make decisions on the extent to which it should become
financially involved and exercise control over various aspects
of distribution.

21. Distribution: control considerations. Major factors to
be considered are as follows:

(a) The physical distribution of products including the
maintenance of stock.
(b) Establishing contact with buyers.
(c) Providing information to buyers.
(d) Negotiating sales.
(e) Providing technical advice and after-sales service.

Every country has its established channels of distribution
and the principles governing their selection are as set out in
Chapter IX. It is always wise to study the use of channels
by competitive organisations. Various marketing institutions,
however, provide specialist services in the field of international
marketing in order to reduce the separation between producers
and consumers (*see* I, **8**).

22. Specialist marketing institutions. The following marketing institutions may be used because they have an expertise
not possessed by the producer organisation or because they
enable the producer to enjoy many of the opportunities afforded
in overseas markets at a low level of financial investment and
risk:

(a) *Export merchants.* Goods are purchased outright by the
merchant in the country of origin. The merchant then takes
over the task of re-selling abroad. Use of merchants means
that the manufacturing organisation has no control over

marketing operations. Merchants usually handle many lines and may not attempt to sell aggressively a particular company's products. Non-differentiated commodities, *e.g.* raw copper, may be handled more successfully in this way than products which have distinctive benefits and company and brand identification. Export merchants do, however, offer advantages to small companies lacking resources or knowledge to export directly, or to large companies in small market potential areas. Many export houses provide a wide range of valuable services, *e.g.* information on markets, agents, advertising, finance. Merchants sometimes are also able to carry out more effectively barter arrangements which may be necessary in dealing with countries in the Eastern bloc.

(b) *Overseas company buying offices.* Many large companies establish buying offices abroad. Once an order is placed with an overseas supplier he normally makes arrangements for transportation, invoicing, documentation and so on.

(c) *Export commission houses.* These organisations act as buyers on behalf of overseas companies. They try to locate suitable supply sources, putting buyers and sellers in contact. They are paid in the form of commissions from the foreign firms they represent on the basis of sales ultimately negotiated.

(d) *Overseas agents.* The appointment of overseas agents or distributors has traditionally been a major method of exporting. Historically, British export success has been based very largely on the notion of finding distributors to stock, advertise and sell products and to develop markets at a reasonable margin of profit. Personal contact on the basis of exchange visits was rare and business was transacted almost entirely by correspondence. Unfortunately, this original tenuous arrangement often persists. Agents can still frequently perform a most valuable export selling operation at the minimum risk, but great care must be taken in selection and very considerable attention must be paid to training, motivation, direction, and support.

NOTE: Licensing (**29, 30**) also has the advantages of limited investment and low risk. Methods of international marketing involving much higher risk and investment are examined later (**32–41**).

23. Important factors in selecting agents. Because agents are so widely used it is appropriate to examine in closer detail problems of agency selection, agency agreements (**27**) and methods of motivating agents (**28**). When the decision is taken to use agents it should be realised that these agents will carry the major burden of effective selling, however much support (*e.g.* advertising and technical assistance) they may receive from the company engaging them. Careful selection is, therefore, absolutely essential. Factors to be considered in making the selection are examined in **24** and **25** below.

24. Business standing, reputation and policy. The following points must be taken into account:

(*a*) *Financial strength and reputation* with bankers and suppliers; credit policies.

(*b*) *Business success* or prospects of success. The record of sales growth over the past few years is a valuable selection pointer. Again, the significance of business with a new company would have to be considered. A fairly new agency with the right resources and development potential might sometimes sell more aggressively.

(*c*) *Integrity.* Agents must have a favourable reputation with the trade and be trustworthy in conforming to the spirit of agreements and plans made with the company they represent.

(*d*) *The number and type of products handled.* An agent will be most readily motivated if business with a particular company represents a significant part of his profits. Handling of competitive products or a very long portfolio of products would be most undesirable.

(*e*) *Business and technical competence.* It is important for agents to be able to take decisions quickly and efficiently without constant reference back to the manufacturer at home.

25. Marketing organisation and expertise. The agents' ability must be evaluated through careful consideration of the following:

(*a*) *Marketing strength.* This may be seen in the size and quality of the sales force, the quality and location of warehousing and office facilities, reputation with customers, customer coverage, pricing and advertising policies, knowledge of market and market requirements.

(*b*) *Ability to undertake market research* and to feed back reliable information on market developments. The ability to communicate in appropriate languages is of great importance.

(*c*) *Provision of after-sales service.* This also covers the stocking of spares. Ready availability of replacements, supply continuity and maintenance arrangements are often the key to success.

(d) *Marketing training*. An agent should be willing to co-operate with the home manufacturer in providing suitable training.

26. What agents want from the company. Some of the best agents may already have arrangements with competing companies. They will certainly look for readily marketable products and favourable conditions, *e.g.* commissions, credit, product guarantees, delivery reliability of product and spares, training, advertising support, technical support.

27. Agency agreements. Agreements should normally be kept as simple as possible but very careful consideration must be given to defining certain essential rights which otherwise will possibly lead to dispute.

(a) Duration of the agreement.   There may well be advantages in having the initial trial period reasonably short.

(b) Exclusiveness or otherwise of representation.   Agents will naturally aim at exclusive representation; suppliers will have to consider the longer-term implications of exclusive rights over wide territories if business develops beyond the capacity of original agents.

(c) Payment, discount, tax conditions.

(d) Delivery conditions.

(e) Rights to additional or new products.

(f) Pricing policy.

(g) Use of trade names, trademarks, etc.

(h) Advertising, promotion and sales literature requirements.

(i) Inventory holding.

(j) Reports and information exchange.

It should be noted that often the law affords greater protection to the agent than to the overseas supplier.

28. Stimulating agents. Personal visits by home company executives to sole agents should be arranged on a fairly frequent basis.   These should not be purely a matter of courtesy but be sufficiently long to measure progress and offer help and suggestions—generally to motivate and tactfully control. Some companies engage field forces (not always large—but highly mobile) who work with, train and motivate agents. Return visits by agency personnel not only create a sense of belonging but provide opportunities for technical and sales training.   Some companies have found that sales conferences of agents have generated tremendous enthusiasm and provided an invaluable means of exchange of ideas.   Many companies find that sales targets provide a major incentive.   Rewards can take various forms, *e.g.* special pricing structure, additional promotional support.   One problem is to establish and agree realistic targets.   Potential must be be taken into consideration —not simply past performance.   If precise market data is lacking, potentials can often be established with adequate accuracy by using combinations of indicators, *e.g.*:

(a) *per capita* Gross National Product;
(b) percentage of Gross National Product accounted for by wholesaling and retailing;
(c) economic development status;
(d) literacy rate;
(e) percentage of population in towns and cities;
(f) industrial output;
(g) average household size;
(h) import volume and pattern;
(i) population statistics.

A regular flow of well-planned bulletins, letters, publicity (*see* VII, **33**) and promotional ideas should be maintained to keep interest high.

29. Licensing.   (*See* **22**, NOTE.)   Licensing takes various forms, *e.g.* patent design or process licence contracts, trademark contracts, technical information contracts, franchising contracts.

The exporting of expertise, which can be extremely rewarding, is a very underdeveloped area of British international trading.   It is often the fastest way of entering overseas markets—sometimes the only possible way, *e.g.* in centrally planned economies.   It is clearly a method involving little expense, avoiding all distribution cost.   On the other hand, it may not be the best way of maximising on overseas opportunities in the long run and there is a risk of creating potentially serious competition.   At this point it should be noted that, frequently, successful international operations depend on a combination of the exporting methods best suited to particular

G

markets at particular points of time in relation to company policy and development plans.

30. Major reasons for entering into licencing agreements.
A major reason for entering into licensing agreements is that no capital risk is involved. There are, however, other considerations as follows:

(a) Licensing arrangements normally involve close collaboration and, at a later stage, more direct involvement may be possible and desirable.

(b) Cross-licensing arrangements may be easier to negotiate. This is particularly important in view of the high cost of specialised research and development and the speed of scientific and technological change. Licensing arrangements can be used to obtain a higher return on the costs of research investment.

(c) Currency advantages exist as foreign currency is saved and there are few exchange difficulties.

(d) Some markets are too small or too risky for any serious consideration of capital investment.

(e) Licensees often have well-developed marketing organisations.

(f) Licensing may overcome the barriers of trading with nationally owned enterprises or of trading in countries with strong nationalist tendencies. Newly established or developing countries, for example, may accept licensing agreements as a means of stimulating economic development without the risk of foreign domination of industries and markets.

(g) The customer reputation created through some licensing arrangements may assist in the marketing of other company products currently or later.

(h) There are advantages in diversifying the methods of receiving income from overseas.

31. Problems to be considered.

(a) *Long-term risks.* Apart from the obvious problem of weighing risk against opportunity, licensing involves a number of potential dangers which must be seriously considered. It is important, for example, that there should be adequate safeguards for the maintenance of quality standards if a company's reputation is not to suffer. Companies with large financial resources must consider the long-term position most carefully. Patents and trademarks are valid for a limited period of time only and, if the real long-term aim is to enter more directly into overseas operation, the licensing period may have provided just the necessary time for the licensee to acquire the skills and marketing position with which it would be difficult—and certainly costly—to compete.

(b) *Legal factors.* Licensing agreements require specialist legal advice. They will often, in any case, require the approval of governments, but in the final analysis there has to be complete mutual confidence. It is now very rare for a company simply to agree to a set fee; almost invariably royalty payments based on the value of the business are built into the agreement, which may also contain provisions for the possibility of acquiring equity, termination arrangements, minimum volume conditions, renewal conditions, taxation and accounting procedures, degree of exclusiveness, sub-contracting rights.

32. Joint venture. Joint venture involves a capital partnership and may be arranged in connection with manufacturing activities, marketing activities or both. The case for and against joint venture is considered in **33–36** below.

33. Advantages of joint venture.

(a) *Political.* Like licensing, this is frequently a method which is acceptable to governments who strictly limit imports or the operations of wholly-owned foreign companies. Local conditions may regulate the extent of such co-operation but, once established, joint ventures usually receive favourable treatment in matters of import licences, taxation and exchange control.

(b) *Financial.* Joint ventures are often regarded as the safest, easiest and least expensive method of engaging in international business. It may be possible to obtain local capital which is a safeguard against the risks of political and economic instability.

(c) *Commercial.* These may include acquiring new knowledge on manufacturing methods or research information. Access to new markets may be gained through a well-established distribution system.

34. Problems of joint venture. The most important ultimate consideration is probably the amount of control which can be exercised over the vital decision-making processes. Some companies will not enter into joint venture agreements unless they have a majority financial interest. Differences in management philosophy, cultural attitudes, development plans or dividend policy, for example, may lead to considerable strife and possible deadlock. Legal agreements have to be supplemented by a tremendous amount of mutual confidence.

35. Major preliminary requirements. To minimise the risk of later difficulties there should be:

(a) a thorough investigation of the contributions the parties can make to research, manufacturing or marketing expertise, plant facilities and equipment, and so on;

(b) a clear understanding of exactly what is required from the partners;

(c) a clear understanding of profit pay-out policy, e.g. long-term investment at low returns or high immediate returns.

36. Decision-making in joint venture. Companies operating on a world-wide basis may find special problems in joint venture arrangements, particularly in relation to pricing and supply. Single ownership allows for the setting of corporate company objectives, profit standards and use of resources. Joint venture decisions cannot be based on the same premises.

37. Wholly-owned subsidiaries. Overseas companies may be involved in the whole commercial process from design through to manufacturing and marketing, or they may concentrate on a particular operation, e.g. purchasing, marketing or manufacturing, or the manufacture or assembly of parts. Whatever the extent of the operation, there is complete capital commitment and control.

The decision to invest in overseas establishments is normally the result of either failure to find a suitable alternative or belief that complete company control is essential for the most effective and profitable operation. It is large companies who usually move in this direction, but small and medium-sized companies might be wise to consider the possibilities since the investment need not necessarily be very high. The recovery of initial investment, however, may be comparatively slow and it is the long-term advantages which should be taken into account. Statements that exporting is unprofitable often arise from short-term thinking. A substantial world business may be highly profitable, but time for build-up will certainly be needed.

38. Establishing overseas companies. There are two basic methods: acquisition, and starting from scratch. Special factors which may lead to foreign ownership include the following:

(a) *The volume of business expected.* This is very frequently the principal criterion in establishing overseas sales branches.

(b) *The need to provide specialised facilities.* It may be very important to establish adequate servicing, by way of spare parts, repair facilities, and so on.

(c) *The strength of nationalistic feeling.* This may be reflected in official government policy by the provision of financial incentives, tax or exchange benefits, but it may also be a matter of potential buyer sentiments. Customers may sometimes react more favourably to products which are produced in their own country. In consumer goods in particular, customers are frequently unaware that the producing company is foreign.

(d) *Reduction of manufacturing overheads.* Domestic plant capacity may be of such size that it is essential to have large world markets and the establishment of overseas sales branches may lead to a more profitable total operation, even if these branches are not highly profitable in their own right.

(e) *Legal restrictions.* Prohibitive import duties or conditions, severe exchange restriction or heavy tax burdens can sometimes be overcome. Sometimes it is necessary to establish an overseas operation in order to exercise a patent.

(f) *Rationalisation.* Ownership may lead to more profitable overall global operations by rationalisation of manufacturing, research, servicing and/or marketing activities.

(g) *Capital availability.* Overseas development may offer advantages in the re-investment of profits or the raising of capital from local sources. In many cases long-term credit is easier to finance—and this is particularly important in the marketing of capital equipment.

(h) *Advantages in acquiring particular currencies* which may be transferable to other overseas operations.

39. Risk factors. The extent of risk will obviously depend on the size of the investment, which may be small in the case of establishing sales, purchasing or warehousing facilities, or very large in the setting up of a large assembly or manufacturing plants. A major consideration will be the possibility of loss in the case of nationalisation. A marketing operation may incur a high running cost in terms of salaries, but large-scale investment in fixed assets—manufacturing installations and equipment, for example—is a much greater cause for investigation of stability of government policy. Nationalisation is not the only problem. Currency and exchange-rate stability are important considerations.

40. Problems of acquisition. Although acquisition may seem an attractive means of developing overseas trade on a large scale quickly it is important that any acquisition should be preceded by the formulation of a clear policy and a thorough investigation of the business to be acquired:

(a) *A clear acquisition policy.* In order to develop a truly international business most profitably it will often be necessary to co-ordinate policy and rationalise resources. Heterogeneous acquisitions make these steps virtually impossible. The American General Foods organisation encountered enormous difficulties after acquiring businesses in many parts of the world on the very general basis of involvement in convenience foods markets. Convenience foods are difficult to define on a global basis. This raises problems of product policy which have direct repercussions on development and research. Many other problems arise from divergencies in accounting systems, personnel policy, business philosophy and so forth.

(b) *A careful investigation of the business to be acquired.* Investigations must be made to discover the following:

    (i) Financial standing and profitability record.

    (ii) Market standing and marketing organisation and methods.

    (iii) Personnel policies and, in particular, wage and salary structures.

    (iv) Research and development strengths or weaknesses.

    (v) Patents and licensing agreements.

    (vi) Plant and depot facilities and values.

    (vii) The strength and weaknesses in the existing management structure. This is a particularly important issue since a great deal will depend on the ability and adaptability of the local management team.

    (viii) Government regulations and controls.

Many companies use the services of brokers or consultants in locating suitable companies for acquisition. Really good prospects are difficult to find and an extensive search may well be necessary. The use of legal and financial specialists will clearly be necessary in evaluating possible acquisitions, but other management personnel, *e.g.* research, manufacturing, marketing, will usually be needed to carry out a complete investigation.

41. Organisation structure. It is usually impracticable—and unwise—to think in terms of setting up an organisational structure which is a replica of the home operation.   There may be very real differences in market conditions, effective manufacturing methods, administrative procedures, growth rate and personnel capability.   There are very few companies which have as yet succeeded in creating a fully integrated international operation—one which has no dominant domestic roots, but which is fully international in ownership, financing, management and operation.   There is little doubt that such companies will increasingly emerge in the future.

The problems of corporate organisational structure are enormous.   It is clear that there must be some degree of central control—but the problem is to determine the extent of that control, to establish the appropriate relationships between central staff and line management and decentralised managements.

The following are some of the questions that need to be posed:

(*a*) To what extent, for example, does central planning and direction conflict with the development of a decentralised profit responsibility concept?   What type of reporting system is needed?

(*b*) How is it possible to utilise the best managerial talent in the right place at the right time?   To what extent is it possible to think in terms of truly multi-national management structures? How can the problems of differences in standards and cost of living be overcome if management is to be moved from one operation to another?

(*c*) What should be the basis of evaluating the performance of different companies, considering the wide differences which exist in, for example, government taxation systems, currency stability, market structures and development problems, and cost factors?

(*d*) What special qualities are needed in the international manager and how can he be trained and developed?

(*e*) To what extent should immediate or local considerations outweigh long-term and corporate considerations in determining the allocation of resources?

42. The international manager. Special qualities and/or qualifications are needed in the personnel selected to carry out operations. Far too little consideration has been given to providing the training and development programmes needed for British personnel working in overseas territories.

Overseas operations demand the following qualities:

(a) *The capacity and authority to make prompt decisions.* Overseas buyers are not likely to react favourably to men who have constantly to refer back to headquarters. Even an overseas representative will need to be much more capable of assuming responsibility of a managerial kind than his counterpart in home markets. He may well be responsible for guiding agency operations as well as for direct customer dealings.

(b) *Adaptability.* This characteristic is needed to cope with the wider range of unusual conditions surrounding the transaction of business.

(c) *Knowledge of languages.* The importance of language is too often underrated because of the ability of other nations to communicate reasonably well in English.

(d) *Acceptance of the need for mobility.* The distances which may have to be covered and the possibility of international transfers make it essential that wives and families are prepared to adjust to a particular way of life. It may be necessary to provide special incentives to cover the possible additional cost of education, travel, home visits.

(e) *Health and energy.* Overseas operations are usually more demanding physically than domestic operations.

(f) *Knowledge of local customs,* culture and current events.

(g) *Tolerance*—a willingness to recognise that people with different cultural backgrounds have different points of view which to them are as valid as any other; an ability to work with and through people with diverse attitudes, beliefs and motivations.

(h) *Persistence.* It may frequently be necessary to pursue a line of action for a long time in face of difficulties before success is finally achieved.

(i) *Reliability and attention to details.* Irritations and business loss may spring from slow, inaccurate or vague transmission of information. Weaknesses in administrative procedures leading to delivery delays, excessive correspondence or slow reaction to complaints intensify the doubts an organisation may have of doing business at all with overseas companies.

Whatever the form of overseas operations it is clear that success depends to a very large extent on the calibre of the personnel involved, and there must be an acceptance that this usually means that top-level executives must themselves be more mobile and more directly in touch with the market place.

43. Organisational evolution. It is beyond the scope of this book to cover all the various organisational structures to be found in practice. A small export operation run entirely through agents may, at the outset, be organised by a small section of the home marketing department. This may develop into a separate export division with responsibility for market investigations, distribution systems, service, advertising and promotion. The establishment of overseas sales offices, assembly points and warehouses may follow. As the organisation develops, problems of communication and the relationship with the home operation will have to be resolved. The final step, is the creation of a fully international corporation.

MARKETING SERVICES AND GOVERNMENT SUPPORT

44. The need for international marketing research. The differences in social, economic, technical, political and legal systems (12–16 above) and in distribution patterns (17–20 above) clearly point to the need for particular attention to be paid to marketing research and promotion. The geographical separation of producers and consumers adds to the normal marketing problems of separation of time and knowledge or information (see I, 8).

45. International marketing research: the basic steps. There are really four major steps in an investigation. These are as follows:

(a) Basic data concerning the market.
(b) General factors relating to the product.
(c) Specific factors relating to the market for the product.
(d) Specific factors which would influence the operation of the particular company.

46. Major problems to be resolved. The first two steps of an investigation are required for top-level policy decisions in connection with involvement in overseas areas. The third and fourth steps are required for decisions on distribution outlets, prices, terms and so on, but, more important, on specific products need to suit specific markets. For product decisions information on the following will be necessary:

(a) The effect of differing legal requirements.

(b) The advantages and disadvantages of standardisation of complete products or components.

(c) The need to adapt existing products to suit local conditions, functional or aesthetic design changes, packaging, branding and advertising, quality standards, and specifications.

47. Special problems in conducting overseas surveys. The techniques covered in Chapter III apply but the following are some of the special problems which may arise:

(a) *The choice of the means of undertaking investigations: e.g.* overseas agencies, British agencies, agencies with international associations, company staff. The major problem is to weigh up the frequently conflicting considerations of efficiency, time and cost. A provisional estimate of a market may be prepared by experienced researchers in two or three days whereas a more detailed investigation may require two or three months, including time for preparation of the survey, for execution, and for analysis and interpretation. Field interviewing can clearly involve high travelling expenses.

(b) *The value of published information.* Information from every possible source should be utilised, but it varies in reliability and statistics are often constructed on differing bases.

(c) *Language problems.* Large companies' executives may speak English, but surveys may need to cover respondents who are not bilingual. If the researchers cannot speak the particular language, interpreters have to be used, raising questions of additional cost and communication difficulties.

(d) *Terminology.* Definitions and technical specifications in connection with similar products may be widely divergent.

(e) *Differences in culture and traditions.* These may affect the willingness of respondents to co-operate and the reliability of the answers they give.

48. Selection of advertising agencies and media. Important matters to consider are the following:

(a) *Choice of agency.* As in marketing research there are very large international companies and local companies of various sizes; there is also the possibility of using a British-based agency. The range and efficiency of services offered requires most careful consideration.

(b) *Differences in the quality and quantity* of media available. Contrast the availability of commercial television, national daily press, magazines and trade literature, for example, in France, the USA, Germany and Britain. Accurate statistics on circulation and readership are often difficult to obtain.

(c) *Direct mailing.* This is a form of presentation which is receiving increasing attention. Obvious difficulties arise in obtaining full and classified lists of potential overseas customers. Direct mailing can often be most effectively organised in co-operation with local agents.

49. Economic and social problems in promotion. Differences in economic and social systems (*see* **13, 14** above) create individual promotion problems. Some of these problems are considered in **50–54** below.

50. Level of expenditure. The stage of economic development reached has a direct bearing on the extent of advertising. Highly developed economies, as might be expected, show a higher level of advertising expenditure than underdeveloped economies but the level of expenditure is not directly related to either national income or *per capita* income. In general, however, companies should be prepared to spend comparatively more on advertising in overseas than in domestic markets since both they and their products will usually be less well known and have less intensive direct selling effort.

51. Distribution patterns. Differences in distribution patterns (*see* **17** above) may mean that there should be a totally different allocation of advertising expenditure; *e.g.* if final distribution is mainly in the hands of small retailers it may be difficult to obtain effective displays but profitable to concentrate on promotions to large wholesalers.

52. Differences in customer motivations. Buying habits will be conditioned by income and assets available but there will be differences in priorities and values. European countries with strong Protestant traditions tend to resist appeals based on labour saving, for example. Reports from many sources show that Swiss housewives reacted much more favourably to dish-washing machines promoted essentially on the basis of high water temperatures and sterilisation than on the basis of ease and convenience.

53. Differences in decision-makers. The influence of women and children differs tremendously in consumer goods markets. In industrial markets, management structure and styles have to be considered in determining the form and direction of communications.

54. International "images." There are obvious advantages in terms of both cost and effectiveness if a company can use the same kind of advertising copy and visual material all over the world. It is, however, rarely possible to reproduce indentical promotional material for different markets. There are problems in translation but illustrations must often be modified or completely changed; *e.g.* a Smarties advertisement showing children physically handling the sweets and examining their different colours was completely unacceptable in Holland because of the Dutch attitude towards hygiene. Agents and distributors can often provide invaluable help in advising on idiomatic usage and appropriateness of copy and visual appeal.

NOTE: Legal regulations differ. Particular attention will need to be paid to restrictions in the advertising of food and drugs.

55. Exhibitions. The decisions to participate in home exhibitions is not infrequently based on the notion of keeping in line with competitive practice rather than on calculated objectives in regard to communications and sales. Overseas exhibitions often attract much more serious buying attention and may be one of the most effective ways of communicating with potential customers. It is important to plan for exhibitions well in advance. The most important should be carefully selected and a timetable not only of the events themselves but of preparatory work must be drawn up. Apart from important matters of stand design, location and size, it will be necessary to prepare special literature and exhibits and to allocate responsible executives. The Board of Trade provides valuable advice and assistance to British companies wishing to take part in international exhibitions. In addition,

through its Overseas Fairs Directorate, the Board of Trade
organises British Pavilions and Information Stands and All-
British Trade Fairs. British Weeks are also organised and
financed by the Board of Trade and assistance is given in
promoting British goods through special store promotions.

56. Co-operation in exporting. The cost of overseas marketing operations sometimes prevents companies from undertaking activities in which they could effectively participate
if they were to look more closely at the possibilities of collaboration. Manufacturers' associations or voluntary groupings
of firms could achieve great economies by co-operative effort
in organising exhibitions, advertising, selling missions or
visits by buyers. Co-operation in industrial markets may be
necessary to supply a complete system, *e.g.* the building of
oil refineries and power plants. Special consortia are sometimes set up for combined tenders. The Board of Trade can
assist and/or advise in all these matters and, for the smaller
manufacturer, there is the "pick-a-back" scheme which enables
firms to contact successful exporting organisations who are
willing to assist by offering certain selling facilities. The
Institute of Marketing has established a company, Marketing
Ltd., specifically to arrange for co-operative export marketing
efforts.

57. Credit and insurance. Exporters face not only normal
commercial risks of payment default but the additional risks
of shifting political circumstances, currency exchange and
import restrictions. There is also, in increasingly competitive
world markets, the problem of providing long-term credit.
Most exporters have, therefore, to obtain finance from outside
sources which themselves require reasonable guarantees
against risk. Various national schemes have been developed
in most industrialised countries to assist in the problems of
credit and risk. Some schemes are private; others are state
controlled (*cf.* Hermes Kreditversicherungs A.G., Hamburg—
a private company—and the Export Risks Insurance Corporation Ltd., Bombay—a government-owned corporation).

58. The Export Credit Guarantees Department. The British
Government has established an Export Credit Guarantees
Department at the Board of Trade. *Board of Trade Export*

Handbook Number 2 (1967) sets out the main features and conditions of the scheme. It is possible to insure from the date of contract acceptance or from the date of the shipment. There are comprehensive policies covering the whole of a company's business or export business, and specific policies for particular large individual export contracts.

(*a*) *Rates.* These vary according to the extent of risk involved and cover requested. Rates for special contracts, for example, are higher than those for comprehensive policies. Even special policy rates are, however, favourable. For example, premiums on a contract on five years' instalment credit with a substantial pre-delivery period would range from approximately £1·25 to £4 per £100. There is also a specially attractive introductory scheme for the new small exporter. Maximum coverage is normally for 90 or 95% but, in special cases, 100% cover may be offered.

(*b*) *Cover.* ECGD cover provides the necessary collateral for normal bank financing and various special guarantees to banks may also be negotiated. The main risks for which cover may be provided are:

    (*i*) insolvency of buyer;
    (*ii*) failure of buyer to pay within six months of acceptance of goods;
    (*iii*) war, civil wars, revolutions;
    (*iv*) cancellation of UK export licences or new export restrictions;
    (*v*) delay in the transfer of sterling to the UK.

59. The Diplomatic Service. It should be remembered that the Diplomatic Service through its commercial services is increasingly devoting attention to the promotion of exports by providing market information, advising on overseas opportunities and assisting in liaison between British and overseas companies and trade organisations.

60. Conclusion. It is evident that increasing home competition, the profit squeeze, increasing world industrialisation, and the formation of economic trading communities will all combine to bring pressure on the need for consideration of marketing on an international basis. The distinction between home and export business will tend to disappear and marketing strategies will be based on global rather than national patterns or segmentations.

The principles of marketing set out in Chapters I–X are as true of international as of home markets. Decisions have to be made on product policy, pricing, promotion, channels and organisation. Customers have to be understood, forecasts and targets have to be set and performance has to be measured. Special knowledge and means of obtaining that knowledge are, however, required. Thus special training and experience must be linked with appropriate adaptability to environment and linguistic ability. Not least important is the fact that company directors and top-level executives must become committed to accepting the marketing philosophy and to more personal involvement in the actual fields of operation.

PROGRESS TEST 12

1. What are the most significant recent trends in international trade? (3–7)

2. What basic information is needed to analyse world market opportunities? (11)

3. In what basic ways do international markets differ? (12–20)

4. What specialist marketing institutions might be used by a company seeking entry to overseas markets at a low level of risk and investment? (22).

5. List the important factors to be considered in selecting agents. (23–25)

6. What are the major reasons for entering into licensing agreements? (30)

7. Why and how do companies establish wholly-owned subsidiaries? (37, 38)

8. What are the main problems involved in the acquisition of overseas companies? (40)

9. What special qualities does the "international" manager require? (42)

10. What are the special problems of international marketing research? (47)

11. What are the economic and social problems of international promotion? (49–54)

12. What is the function of the Export Credit Guarantees Department of the Board of Trade? (58)

EXTERNAL SOURCES OF MARKETING INFORMATION

THERE are many external sources of information; the more important can be categorised as follows:

GOVERNMENT PUBLICATIONS

Census of Population. The last full Census was carried out in 1961 but a 10% sample census was taken in 1966. The Census supplies details of population by age, marital status, occupation, social class, house ownership, sex, geographical area and a considerable amount of social and economic data. This can be supplemented by the annual statistics produced by the General Register Office.

Statistics on Incomes, Prices, Employment and Production. The Department of Employment and Productivity publishes a bulletin several times per year and this is supplemented in the monthly *Gazette*. Details of employment and unemployment by industry and region, data on wage rates and retail prices, industrial disputes, etc., provide useful guides to purchasing potential by areas and income groups. More detailed analyses of incomes are available from Inland Revenue statistics.

Annual Family Expenditure Surveys. These are carried out by the Department of Employment and Productivity and give details of consumer spending on individual items by income groups and geographical areas. The survey is based on a limited sample of some 3000 households.

Census of Distribution. These were carried out by the Board of Trade in 1950, 1957, 1961 and 1966. The 1950 and 1961 surveys involved a complete analysis of distribution through retail outlets. The 1957 and 1966 surveys were only partial.

Census of Production. This census, carried out every five years, gives information on manufacturing organisations, mining and quarrying, building and contracting and public utilities. The information includes details of materials and fuel purchased, stocks at the beginning and end of a year, annual output and sales analysis, expenditure on services, plant, machinery and vehicles, and value of buildings and land. Calculations of gross output, net output and net output per person employed are made.

Monthly Digest of Statistics. This contains information collected by various government departments, *e.g.* Board of Trade, Ministry of Technology, Ministry of Power. The information is summarised in the *Annual Abstract of Statistics.*

The Board of Trade Business Monitor Series. This gives monthly or quarterly data on production over a wide range of industries as well as comparisons with past figures.

Overseas Trade Accounts. These are published monthly by the Customs and Excise Department, showing, in detail, figures on imports and exports.

Statistical Classification for Imported Goods and Re-exported Goods.

Annual Statement of Trade of the UK with Commonwealth and Foreign Countries.

Trade and Navigation Accounts. These are published monthly by the Board of Trade.

The Export Service Bulletin. Published by the Board of Trade.

Board of Trade Journal.

UK Balance of Payments and the Economic Report.

Input-Output Tables for the UK. These are designed to show the flow of business from one industry to another, and cover industrial groupings.

Public Investment in Great Britain.

Directory of Employers' Associations, Trade Unions and Joint Organisations.

Company Assets, Income and Finance. This is published by the Board of Trade and shows the net assets, profits, reserves and new capital of over 2000 companies.

National Income and Expenditure Blue Book. Although all the raw statistics appear elsewhere the data is processed in this annual publication to provide a particularly valuable source of social and economic information for both consumer and industrial marketing.

Special surveys published by the Social Survey Unit of the Central Office of Information.

The above publications are available from H.M.S.O. and students should consult the *List of Principal Statistical Series Available*, published by H.M.S.O.

OFFICIAL INTERNATIONAL PUBLICATIONS

United Nations Statistical Year Book.
United Nations Monthly Bulletin of Statistics.
United Nations Current Economic Indicators.
United Nations World Economic Survey.
United Nations Commodity Trade Statistics.
Bulletin of the European Economic Community.

EFTA Bulletin.
Statistics for Market Research in Europe and North America (Organisation for Economic Co-operation and Development).
Bulletin Générale de Statistiques (European Economic Commission).
International Monetary Statistics (International Monetary Fund).

OTHER SPECIALIST PUBLICATIONS

Quarterly Economic Reviews⎫
Retail Business   ⎬*Economist* Intelligence Unit.
Marketing in Europe   ⎭
A. C. Nielsen Indices—for food, drugs, pharmaceuticals, confectionery and tobacco.
Legion Publishing Company's *Statistical Review of Advertising Expenditure.*
Bradstreet Register.
Dun and Bradstreet's Guide to Key British Enterprises.
Kompass Register.
Stock Exchange Year Book.
Kelly's Directory of Merchants, Manufacturers and Shippers.

NEWSPAPERS, PERIODICALS AND JOURNALS (* = American).

The London and Cambridge Economic Bulletin.
The Times Review of Industry and Technology.
The Economist.
The Financial Times.
The Statist.
British Journal of Marketing.
Marketing.
Marketing Forum.
Commentary.
Scientific Business.
*Journal of Marketing.**
*Journal of Marketing Research.**
*Journal of Advertising Research.**
*Harvard Business Review.**
Reviews published by the various banks.

INSTITUTIONS

The Institute of Marketing, Richbell Place, Lamb's Conduit Street, London W.C.1.
The British Market Research Society, 39 Hertford Street, London W.1.
The Advertising Association, 1 Bell Yard, London W.C.2.
The Incorporated Society of British Advertisers, 45 Hertford Street, London W.1.

The Institute of Public Relations, 20 Lamb's Conduit Street, London W.C.1.

The Marketing Society, 8 Clifden House, Windmill Road, Brentford, Middlesex.

The British Institute of Management, Management House, Parker Street, London W.C.2.

The Confederation of British Industry, 21 Tothill Street, London S.W.1.

British National Export Council, 6–14 Dean Farrar Street, London S.W.1.

The Institute of Export, Export House, 14 Hallam Street, London W.1.

Council of Industrial Design, 28 Haymarket, London S.W.1.

British Export Houses Association, 69 Cannon Street, London E.C.4.

British Standards Institute, 2 Park Street, London W.1.

Board of Trade, Export Intelligence and Statistical and Market Intelligence Library, Hillgate House, 35 Old Bailey, London E.C.4.

Central Office of Information, Hercules Road, Westminster Bridge Road, London S.E.1.

H.M. Stationery Office, Atlantic House, Holborn Viaduct, London E.C.4.

Trade Associations.

Chambers of Commerce.

Banks.

Embassies and Consulates.

APPENDIX II

BIBLIOGRAPHY

GENERAL

The Development of Marketing Thought (Bartels). Irwin.

Marketing for Profit (Hardy). Longmans.

Marketing Management (Giles). 2nd edition. Macdonald & Evans.

Marketing Management: Analysis, Planning and Control (Kotler). Prentice-Hall.

Marketing Strategy and Functions (Kelley). Prentice-Hall.

Marketing Systems: An Introductory Analysis (Fisk). Harper International.

The Practice of Marketing (Smallbone). Staples.
Theory in Marketing (Cox, Alderson and Shapiro). Irwin.

CONSUMER BEHAVIOUR

Customer Behaviour and the Behavioural Sciences: Theories and Applications (Ed. Britt). Wiley.
How British Industry Buys (Buckner). Hutchinson.
Human Behaviour in Marketing (Douglas, Field and Tarpey). Merrill.
Industrial Purchasing Behaviour: A Study of Communication Effects (Levitt). Harvard School of Business Administration.
Motivation and Market Behaviour (Ferber and Wales). Irwin.
Social Psychology (Kretch, Crutchfield and Ballachey). McGraw-Hill.

PRODUCT STRATEGY

Developing a Product Strategy. American Management Association.
Innovation in Marketing (Levitt). McGraw-Hill.
The Management of Innovation (Burns and Stalker). Tavistock.
New Product Decisions (Pessemier). McGraw-Hill.
Pricing: The Critical Decision. American Management Association.
Product Strategy and Management (Berg and Schuchman). Holt, Rinehart & Winston.

MARKETING RESEARCH

Industrial Marketing Research: Management and Technique (Stacey and Wilson). Hutchinson.
Marketing Research (Alevizos). Prentice-Hall.
Marketing Research (Crisp). McGraw-Hill.
The Measurement of Meaning (Osgood, Suci and Tannenbaum). University of Illinois.
Motivation Research and Marketing Management (Newman). Harvard School of Business Administration.
Sample Design in Business Research (Deming). Wiley.

ADVERTISING

Advertising and Competition (Telser). Institute of Economic Affairs.
Advertising Procedure (Kleppner). 4th edition. Prentice-Hall.
Industrial Advertising (Messner). McGraw-Hill.
Measuring Advertising Effectiveness (Lucas and Britt). McGraw-Hill.

Modern Advertising Law (Langdon-Davies)   Business Publications.

Promotional Strategy (Engel, Wales and Warshaw).   Irwin.

SALES MANAGEMENT

Control of the Field Sales Force (Smallbone).   Staples.
The Field Sales Manager.   American Management Association.
Management of the Sales Force (Stanton and Buskirk).   Irwin.
Sales Administration: Principles and Problems (Canfield).   Prentice-Hall.
The Sales Manager's Handbook (Apsley and Harkness).   Dartnell.
Selling to Industry.   British Institute of Management.

MARKETING CONTROL

Business Budgeting and Control (Herkert and Willson).   Ronald Press.
Cost Problems in Modern Marketing (Kjaer).   Hansen: North Holland.
Financial Management of the Marketing Function (Schiff and Mellman).   Financial Executives Research Foundation, New York.
Marketing and the Computer (Alderson, Roe and Shapiro).   Prentice-Hall.
Marketing Productivity Analysis (Sevin).   McGraw-Hill.
New Decision-Making Tools for Managers (Bursk and Chapman).   New English Library.

CHANNELS OF DISTRIBUTION

The Changing Pattern of Distribution (Stacey and Wilson).   Hutchinson.
Competition for Consumers (Fulop).   Institute of Economic Affairs.
Costs and Competition in Retailing (McClelland).   Blackwell.
Studies in Retailing (McClelland).   Blackwell.
Supermarketing (Charvat).   Macmillan, New York.
Wholesaling in Marketing Organisations (Revzan).   Wiley.

INTERNATIONAL MARKETING

Board of Trade *Handbooks*, 1, 2 and 3.
Handbook of International Marketing (Stanley).   McGraw-Hill.
International Handbook of Advertising (Ed. Dunn).   McGraw-Hill.
Management of International Operations (Fayerweather). McGraw-Hill.
Market Research on a European Scale.   Organisation for European Economic Co-operation.

Penetrating the International Market (Stuart). American Management Association.

CASE STUDIES

Case Studies in Marketing (Giles). Macdonald & Evans.
International Marketing: Text and Cases (Leighton). McGraw-Hill.
Problems in Marketing (Brown, England and Matthews). McGraw-Hill.

APPENDIX III

EXAMINATION TECHNIQUE

1. Timing. Read the instructions relating to the question to be attempted most carefully. Be sure that you understand how marks are to be allocated. In some papers there is a compulsory question; in others questions are divided into sections in order to ensure that students attempt questions covering as wide a range of the prescribed syllabus as possible. Having understood the directions, read the questions through once fairly quickly. At this stage it is normal for students to become unduly worried. Remember this and read the paper again more slowly, "short-listing" those questions which you believe you can answer most satisfactorily. Then make your final selection in accordance with the instructions given. Deduct a time allowance for reading through your answers at the end of the examination and apportion the remaining time according to the mark contribution each question makes towards the maximum obtainable on the paper. Do not underestimate the cumulative danger of over-running your time allocation for individual questions. Essay-type questions are very rarely awarded full marks and there is almost invariably more to be gained by completing all questions as instructed than by adding small refinements to earlier questions attempted and having insufficient time for later questions.

If you are running out of time make the best of the situation by listing salient points in note form or by covering the overall approach to a problem rather than by writing in full essay form or indulging in specialised calculations affecting a small part of the required answer.

2. Legibility. Examiners are usually marking large numbers of papers. They are not looking for copperplate handwriting but they will naturally be inclined to ignore or be irritated by writing which is difficult to read.

3. Logical presentation.   Written examination questions may occasionally be devised to test knowledge of facts but more usually they are intended to examine the student's ability to use facts in investigating a problem or in analysing a line of argument. It is, therefore, of great importance to plan answers in such a way that they have a logical flow.   Time spent on planning answers is time well spent.

4. Relevance of material.   Read questions carefully and make certain you understand exactly what you are being asked. A lengthy answer is no guarantee of high marks.   Students are apt to write down what they know rather than what they are asked.   This leads to completely irrelevant answers or answers which are out of balance, with undue emphasis being given to particular aspects.

5. Generalisations.   Avoid sweeping and vague generalisations. Be as specific as possible by quoting actual examples, *e.g.* of company organisations, of marketing campaigns, of the statements of writers and practising marketing specialists.

6. Lay-out.   Whenever possible emphasise your key points by suitable paragraph construction, underlining, use of diagrams and statistics.   Clear and accurate diagrams and statistics often enhance an answer and make points more lucidly and rapidly than words, but avoid these devices at all costs if you are unsure of your facts.

7. Style.   If you are a mature student who has not undertaken written examinations for several years it is particularly important to practise written answers in advance of the examination as much as possible.   Write in short, concise sentences, taking care to avoid ambiguous words and phrases.   Define unfamiliar terms and make sure that your use of such terms is consistent.

Except in emergency, do not write in note form.   A definite mark allowance may be made for presentation, but, if not, examiners will normally still expect students to show the ability to express themselves fluently.

8. Assumptions.   In questions requiring analysis of problems it is not unusual for the information supplied to be incomplete. It is expected that assumptions will be made, but that the assumptions will be stated and be maintained consistently throughout.

APPENDIX IV
TEST PAPERS

Do not attempt these papers until you have thoroughly studied the text and can answer satisfactorily the questions in the Progress Tests.

TEST 1

1. By what criteria would you decide whether a company were production or marketing oriented?

2. To what extent would you consider that the purchasing of industrial goods and services is a rational process?

3. Comment on the methods used by companies in determining advertising expenditure. What problems are involved in arriving at a decision and to what extent can these be overcome?

4. Under what conditions is it desirable to eliminate a product? What problems may have to be overcome despite the logic of any arguments put forward?

5. To what extent might channel decisions be conditioned by: (a) the characteristics of the product or products; (b) the practice of competitors? Illustrate your answer by reference to specific companies and products.

6. What would you consider to be the main responsibilities of a field sales manager controlling ten salesmen calling on grocery outlets? What considerations would you have in mind in selecting a man to take up such a position?

7. What do you understand by behavioural sciences? Of what importance is an understanding of behavioural sciences to a marketing research specialist?

8. What political and economic factors would you expect to be examined by a company before a decision is made to invest in setting up its own manufacturing or marketing organisation in an overseas territory?

TEST 2

1. What do you understand by the term "marketing mix"? Comment on the main "mix" differences you might expect to find in marketing plans relating to (a) baby foods and (b) scientific instruments.

2. It is frequently stated that, the longer a man spends as a sales specialist, the less likely he is to develop ultimately into a

good marketing manager. What do you cons.der is the validity of this argument?

3. What are the main problems in determining the size and type of samples for marketing research purposes in (a) specialised industrial markets and (b) mass consumer markets?

4. Discuss the various strategic considerations to be examined in determining a pricing policy. What are the special problems in pricing (a) completely new and differentiated products and (b) minor modifications of existing narrowly differentiated products?

5. To what extent do you consider that existing voluntary controls in advertising provide adequate safeguards for the consumer?

6. What are the problems involved in evaluating the performance of salesmen?

7. What do you understand by the "product life cycle"? What are the advantages of understanding the concept in actual marketing situations?

8. Why do companies frequently appoint sales agents to represent them in international markets? Discuss the problems involved in the selection of agents.

TEST 3

1. "Marketing considerations must receive priority in company strategy and planning, but research and development, manufacturing and finance should have co-equal status with marketing.' Discuss this statement.

2. Discuss the major changes which have taken place in the pattern of retail distribution during the last ten years and the effect these changes have had on the marketing policy of suppliers.

3. By what means is it possible to investigate purchasing behaviour and attitudes which are apparently irrational? What contribution might any findings make in devising a marketing campaign?

4. What procedures would you suggest for determining the priority which might be given to a number of new product possibilities?

5. Comment on the problems of evaluating the effectiveness of advertising. Discuss the significance and limitations of the most commonly used research techniques.

6. Discuss the advantages and disadvantages of licensing and joint venture in international marketing operations.

7. "Relevant timely information is vital for effective marketing control." Discuss this statement indicating the types, sources

and frequency of data which might be required by (*a*) a marketing manager and (*b*) an area sales manager.

8. What are the special factors affecting marketing research investigations in connection with industrial goods and services?

TEST 4

1. "Marketing begins before production and ends after production." Discuss this statement, particularly in the light of company organisational structures.

2. Explain what is meant by the following: (*a*) selective distribution; (*b*) intensive distribution; (*c*) exclusive distribution. Illustrate your answer by discussing distribution strategy in the marketing of (*a*) television receivers; (*b*) surgical appliances; (*c*) shirts; (*d*) motor cycles; (*e*) cigarettes; (*f*) agricultural machinery.

3. "A matching of advertiser needs with media capacity is a pre-requisite to the development of an effective advertising campaign." Examine this requirement in connection with the marketing of (*a*) cars and (*b*) fork-lift trucks.

4. "Cost, ultimately, sets the floor to price." Discuss this statement with particular reference to (*a*) the break-even concept and (*b*) discounted cash flow.

5. What are the objectives of branding products? To what extent is branding feasible and desirable in marketing industrial products?

6. What are the possible benefits of test marketing? What criteria might be used in (*a*) selecting areas and (*b*) determining the period of testing?

7. Why is it important for a company to know as accurately as possible the market share its product enjoys? How can the relevant data be obtained in the case of (*a*) cosmetics and (*b*) industrial detergents?

8. Distinguish between marketing research and marketing intelligence with special reference to the problems of overseas markets.

TEST 5

1. "Marketing calls for a combination of creative and analytical ability." Discuss this statement in connection with the selection of staff in (*a*) a company marketing department and (*b*) an advertising agency.

2. Discuss the advantages and disadvantages of telephone interviews, mail questionnaires and personal interviews in marketing research investigations.

3. Explain the principles involved in "critical path" analysis. Illustrate how the use of C.P.A. might be of value in a particular marketing situation.

4. Comment on the most commonly practised procedures for forecasting sales. What factors would you consider in forecasting the sales of a new car model for a forward period of three years?

5. Discuss the problems of cost allocation in determining marketing budgets.

6. "The pack protects what it sells and sells what it protects." Comment on this double function of packaging with special reference to marketing cake mixes (a) to housewives and (b) to catering organisations.

7. Why is personal direct selling a marked feature of the "marketing mix" in the majority of industrial markets? How might advertising contribute to the accomplishment of the "sales task"?

8. "The more advanced a society, the more it counts the variety of its goods as an indication of the standard of living rather than the amount of those goods." Examine the validity of this statement and the implications it might have on the international marketing plans of a company manufacturing domestic kitchen ware.

TEST 6

1. "Where is our company going? Where should it be going? What is our business, anyway?" Consider the relevance of these three questions posed by T. Levitt of the Harvard Business School to company chief executives in connection with long-term planning and the marketing concept.

2. Discuss the reasons for the emergence of "product" and "brand" managers in larger multi-product companies. Would you expect similar advantages and disadvantages in introducing brand-product management in connection with industrial and consumer markets?

3. Why have many retail organisations promoted "private label" products? How is this development affecting the marketing policies of manufacturers offering products of a similar type?

4. "The fact that the industrial buyer seeks the best value is not tantamount to saying that a seller can never get a high price." Comment on price elasticity in industrial markets and ways in which industrial salesmen may overcome price objections.

5. To what extent do you consider that ability and competence in marketing are transferable? Discuss this question with particular reference to the following suggested transfers:

    (*a*) from industrial products to consumer products selling;

    (*b*) from industrial market research to consumer market research;

    (*c*) from marketing management of consumer goods to marketing management of industrial goods.

    6. Examine the advantages and problems of discounts and credit as forms of buying motivation.

    7. What free external sources of advice and information are available to the manufacturer who wishes to export from the UK?

    8. "Because an individual's values are conditioned by the social class structure he perceives, consumer buying behaviour reflects class differences." Comment on the limitations of the conventional socio-economic class definitions most frequently used in defining market profiles in the light of this statement.

INDEX